CAN AMERICA
SURVIVE ...

As a Democratic Republic
Without Christian Roots?

Freddy Davis

CAN AMERICA SURVIVE … As a Democratic Republic Without Christian Roots? 2nd Edition ©2023 Freddy Davis

First Edition published in 2019 as: The Judeo-Christian Roots of the American Democratic Republic

Copyright 2023 by Leadership Books, Inc,

Book Publisher

Las Vegas, NV – New York, NY

LeadershipBooks.com

ISBN:

978-1-951648-29-9 (Hardcover)

978-1-951648-30-5 (Paperback)

978-1-951648-31-2 (eBook)

For Worldwide Distribution

Printed in USA

Table of Contents

Introduction

I f I have heard it once, I have heard it a thousand times: Judeo-Christian values are not necessary for a democratic republic to operate effectively. But is that in fact true? To answer that question, we must first understand the concept of a Democratic Republic. Just as every religious organization that claims to be Christian is not actually Christian, so too, not every country that claims to be a democratic republic is actually a democratic republic. The truth is, there are numerous countries around the world that even have the term "Democratic Republic" in their name but are neither democratic nor a republic.

A democratic republic, as we speak of it in this book, specifically deals with the form of government that exists in America based on the fundamental foundation of the U. S. Constitution. It is a form of governing where the citizens are responsible for the government's operation by democratically electing representatives to govern on their behalf. Since citizens elect representatives, it is not a pure democracy – as a pure democracy would demand that the citizens vote on everything themselves. At the same time, we do elect our representatives by majority vote, so it is democratic in that sense.

To take that one step further, in America we are also a "Constitutional Republic" – that is, one in which the Constitution is the highest law of the land, and which limits the power of government. So, the question emerges that we want to explore in this book: What do Judeo-Christian values have to do with the existence of a democratic republic? Why would we even consider promoting these kinds of "religious" values as a foundation for operating America's government?

The truth is, every form of governance in existence is based on some set of religious values – even those that claim to be atheistic. It just so happens that the required values for the effective operation of a constitutionally limited democratic republic, such as what exists in America, is Judeo-Christian Theism.

At this point, it is important to understand that Judeo-Christian values did not simply appear out of thin air. They are based on a set of beliefs that have their root in objective reality – that is, they emerge out of the way reality is actually structured. While that may seem, at first glance, to be some kind of philosophical mumbo jumbo, it is not – and the implications of that argument are both profound and practical.

The truth is, there are many people who hold beliefs, and live their lives based on beliefs, that do not reflect reality. This does not mean these people can't go about living normal day-to-day lives. They certainly can. It does mean, however, that as they live their lives there will be times when they think and act in ways that are not logical, true, right, and make no common sense.

What is true on an individual level is also true on a societal level. When a large segment of society believes and acts in ways that do not reflect actual reality, things start going wrong in society. That is when you start seeing things like exceeding amounts of gun violence, racial hatred, political riots, all varieties of sexual immorality, acceptance of abortion as a contraceptive, economic chaos, and the like. And when these untrue beliefs become normalized in society, not only do evil things occur, people also begin to see them as normal and acceptable. That is also the point at which a democratic republic begins to fall apart.

In general terms, a democratic republic is not like other forms of government. This form is specifically designed to maintain order in society based on the moral values of the populace, not of its political leaders. It is the citizenry who are ultimately responsible for the kinds of laws, values, and policies that are put in place by the politicians.

While it is the political class who actually do the work, they are responsible to the citizens who elect them. When the citizens elect people who implement and enforce moral laws and policies, society runs smoothly. When they elect people who promote immoral laws and policies, things start going south – and a democratic republic is not a form of government that will work well in that circumstance.

In modern American society, immoral laws and policies are increasingly prominent, and the result is the kind of massive cultural turmoil we see happening every day. And the root of this turmoil is that a very large segment of society holds beliefs that are immoral, and are electing people who promote and implement those kinds of beliefs.

Before going any further, we need to clarify the concept of "immoral beliefs." Many people, when they consider the word "immoral," think only of sexual behavior. Of course, sexual immorality is a part of the equation, but immorality is a much broader concept than that. Determining what is moral requires that there be some kind of standard by which it can be measured.

Something is moral or immoral based on some objective moral standard. As I use this word, I am asserting that the standard is God's revelation in the Bible. Thus, those who govern based on a different standard are promoting immorality. It must also be noted, however, that those who disagree with my standard are also basing their beliefs on some non-biblical standard, and they think their beliefs are moral and mine are immoral.

So how do we arbitrate this? Is it just a matter of "winner takes all," or is there some objective way to discern what is actually right? Can a democratic republic work if it is based on non-Christian values? This book explores that topic to see if it is possible to come to a definitive conclusion.

Competing Foundations for Defining America's Cultural Morality

The conflict we see happening in modern American society is a worldview war. Many people refer to it as a culture war, but I believe "worldview war" is more appropriate. A worldview is a person's belief about reality (what is real vs. what is fantasy). Now this might seem to some to be a bit strange, or even esoteric. After all it is very difficult to imagine that what you consider to be real could ever be considered not real by other people. But that is exactly the conflict.

Whether it is a person's understanding about God, or the nature of human life, or the most essential priorities of society, people who disagree about these things typically do so at a level that is beyond mere policy. They actually make their arguments based on how they understand the structure of reality. When there are competing visions about what is real and what is fantasy, there are bound to be conflicts – particularly when the competition invades the arena of politics.

The Platforms for Our Beliefs

One of the more interesting aspects concerning an understanding of worldview is that every worldview position is a religious point of view. There are many people who actually don't see the connection between their beliefs and politics, but a connection is always there and this faith element is the foundation for their political beliefs. Some even try to distance themselves completely from a connection with religion by claiming that they are not religious.

That, though, is not the case. In fact, it is impossible for a person to not be religious. The way the objectors try to get around this is by using an explanation of religion that exempts them from the definition; things such as church attendance or participation in social service activities. But that is nothing more than a game of semantics.

In its essence, a religion is a system of beliefs that is based on faith. The fact that a faith system is not associated with some official church, or some organization that is specifically designated as a religious system, does not shield individuals from being associated with a system of beliefs that is based on faith. I often hear people say things like, "I am not religious," or "I don't believe in God," or "I only believe in science," thinking that these statements shield them from being religious. They do not. Every person in existence holds beliefs that are based on faith assumptions – no ifs, ands, or buts about it.

In modern American society, there are two primary conflicting belief systems that are the cause of most of the acrimony: Naturalism and Christian Theism. Naturalism is the belief that the natural universe operating by natural laws is all that exists– there is no supernatural existence. Naturally, people who claim this belief are Atheists (though there are many who claim some kind of religious affiliation but still hold naturalistic beliefs). Often these people say things like,

"A lack of belief is not belief," or "I don't believe anything that can't be proven by science."

But that is not true. Stating one's belief in a negative way does not exempt them from holding a belief. A Naturalist may not believe in God, but does affirmatively believe in something – that the natural universe, operating by natural laws, is all that exists. And a person who says they only believe in what can be proven by science simply does not realize the implications of that statement. Science is a methodology not a belief system, and even Atheists believe in many things that cannot be demonstrated by science.

There are actually four major beliefs that all Naturalists must accept by faith: 1) The universe had a natural origin, 2) life came from non-life, 3) the variety of life forms that exist in the world came into existence by natural processes, and 4) consciousness came from non-consciousness. None of these things can be demonstrated by science, so Naturalists must believe them by faith. Naturalism is, indeed, a belief system.

The primary competing belief to Naturalism in modern American society is Christian Theism. Generic Theism is the belief that there is a transcendent creator God who created the natural universe the way that it currently exists. Christian Theism, then, is Theism that specifically asserts the belief that the real God is the one described in the Bible.

Since the point being made here is that the conflict that exists in modern America is a fight between two competing religious belief systems, it is not necessary to go into more detail about the nature of these systems right now. We will deal with that later. For now, it is enough to know that the worldview war that exists in our current modern society is, in fact, a religious war.

Liberalism vs. Conservatism

The next point we need to grasp is that in modern American society, Liberalism and Conservatism are not merely political points of view. They are the voicing of the two worldviews mentioned above (which are diametrically opposed to one another). And it is the conflicting moral expressions of those worldviews that are being played out in the political arena.

Liberalism

Liberalism (often now referred to as Progressivism), in contemporary America, has its root in a naturalistic worldview. The origin of this worldview belief actually goes back to ancient times. We even see expressions of it in writings that date back to ancient Greece. However, the modern understanding of Naturalism emerged out of the European enlightenment of the 18th and 19th centuries. That was a time when European culture was moving away from a God centered foundation to a man centered one.

The naturalistic worldview framework was greatly advanced when Charles Darwin introduced his Theory of Evolution. This gave those inclined to naturalistic thinking a scientific sounding way to conceive of reality that did not need God. From that base, Naturalism emerged as an increasingly influential belief platform. Politically, it tended to take the form of communism, socialism, progressivism, and other ideological isms that are based upon naturalistic presuppositions.

Naturalism expanded its influence in American culture as the number of people who believed in this worldview concept gradually increased. From the late 1800s through the 1950s, people with this belief foundation increasingly worked their way into important positions within the culture's most influential institutions. By the 1960s, the liberal influence began to dominate in education, the news media, government agencies, business, the entertainment industry, and even in many churches. It was also well established in the nation's political institutions – in all branches and at all levels. Since the 1960s, the influence of Liberalism has only increased.

The expansion of Naturalism has increasingly pushed Theism aside and caused American society to take on an entirely different character from what the founders originally established. As the basic authority source of Naturalism is human reason, those who hold this point of view do not look to the outside authority of a god to provide the basis for personal and societal activity. Rather, these people look to those in positions of societal influence to make the rules.

Those who hold these powerful positions use societal forces, along with their personal preferences, to influence how morality is defined within the culture. Along with that, they understand morality to be relative to current circumstances, rather than absolute based on a revelation from God.

Another important Liberal belief that emerges out of Naturalism is the priority of the collective – as opposed to the individual. Since Liberals believe humans are completely natural animals, they think that the survival of the species, as a collective group, is more important than the development of the individual. Liberals in modern American culture tend to prefer institutional forms that are more consistent with a naturalistic worldview.

The language of Liberalism is expressed in modern culture using the notion of political correctness. Political correctness is the expression of language, ideas, policies, and behavior that attempts to minimize giving offense to others. This kind of language is often found in common speech when speaking of occupation (flight attendant vs. stewardess), gender (firefighter vs. fireman), race (Native American vs. Indian), culture (holiday tree vs. Christmas tree), sexual orientation (gay vs. homosexual), religion (spiritually challenged vs. sinful), disability (intellectually challenged vs. retarded), and age (gerontologically advanced vs. elderly). The purpose of this kind of language is to minimize the differences between individuals in order to create more unity within the collective. Liberals believe doing this promotes the survival of the collective.

Conservatism

America was founded upon a Theistic worldview. The particular form of Theism that underlies Conservatism in America is Christian Theism. Sometimes people refer to this as the Judeo-Christian ethic.

In general terms, Theism has some form of scripture as its primary authority source. It is based on the belief that God has revealed Himself and His ways to mankind. In the case of Christian Theism, the scriptural authority source is specifically the Bible. Not only does this provide the foundation for America's founding moral and social expressions, it also advances the notion of a transcendent authority (God) that people should follow and obey.

Those who initially settled in and developed American society were primarily Europeans who came from a Christian theistic worldview background and believed in the God of the Bible. As such, they established society's various institutions using ideas that came specifically from Christian Theism. Such concepts as the rule of law, freedom of conscience, and the priority of the individual all came from this worldview foundation.

Obviously, these ideas can be codified in law and expressed in the culture in many ways. In the case of America's establishment, the founding fathers intentionally used ideas based on Christian Theism to create the system that now exists in America. It included:

- a constitution (an authoritative, foundational legal document),
- free enterprise (priority of the individual in economic matters),
- federalism (decentralized political power),
- property ownership (priority of the individual regarding land ownership), and
- freedom of religion (free will and freedom of conscience).
- separation of powers (recognition of the corruption that can come with power because of the moral weakness of human beings),

As such, the conservative position, as it relates to American culture, expresses the nation's founding principles. Conservatives are those who hold the point of view that these founding principles are right and should be the basis for societal organization. Conservatives are the people who are working to preserve these principles in modern culture.

Conservatism and Liberalism in the Current American Climate

As we can see, Conservatism and Liberalism are not merely opposing political philosophies. They certainly do include political differences, but the roots go much deeper. On the most fundamental level, they are conflicting worldviews (meaning they represent opposing ways of understanding what is real vs. what is fantasy) that literally contradict each another.

In other words, they are each seeking ways of bringing order to society from differing views of reality that use ideological notions that completely contradict one another. Thus, the culture war battles, that the clash between Conservatism and Liberalism represent, are not merely matters of preference, they are expressions of deeply held religious beliefs.

While Conservatism and Liberalism are not, themselves, religious positions, the worldview foundations they rest upon are fundamentally religious in nature. As such, these expressions will continue to create a great deal of passion and division as they play out in every part of life.

Side by Side Comparison of Conservative and Liberal Values	
Conservative Values (Based on Biblical Theism)	**Liberal Values (Based on Naturalism)**
Man is essentially sinful - The belief, based on a biblical understanding of the nature of mankind, that societal constraints must be in place to lessen the effects of sin.	**Man can build utopia on earth** - The belief, based on the concept of naturalistic evolution, that man has already evolved to a high level and will continue on that path. Social engineering can boost the evolution of the goodness of man.
Natural law - The belief that there are such things as unchanging natural and moral laws that God has established for man to know and follow.	**Positive law** - The belief that man-made laws are responsible for granting rights and/or removing specific privileges from an individual or group. There is no God or inalienable human rights, so humans must make these laws themselves.
Constitutional authority - The belief that there is an overarching authoritative legal framework that is the ultimate foundation for all other laws.	**Human authority** - The belief, based on naturalistic concepts, that the highest authority is man. Those in positions of power within society may create and

This corresponds to the biblical concept of an authoritative document (Scripture) given by God.	alter laws based on their perception of current circumstances.
Free enterprise - The belief, based on biblical teachings, that individuals should work hard and be rewarded for their labor in a free economic environment.	**Economic collectivism** - The belief, based on naturalistic presuppositions, that human survival is the highest value, and equal distribution of resources best promotes that in society.
Individual property ownership - The belief, based on the biblical concept of stewardship and the priority of the individual, that individuals should hold personal property and be responsible to God for its use.	**Collective ownership of property** - The belief, based on the naturalistic concept of the survival of the species and the priority of the collective, that corporate ownership of property best promotes the interests of society.
Freedom of religion - The belief, based on the biblical concept that human beings are free-will creatures created in the image of God, that individuals should be allowed to make decisions regarding religious faith based on freedom of conscience.	**Individual religious belief is subservient to the collective** - The belief, based on the naturalistic concept that human beings are naturally evolved animal creatures, that governmental leadership is best able to decide what beliefs best promote the survival of the collective.
Federalism - The belief, based on the biblical concept of the sinfulness of man and the priority of the individual,	**Centralized federal authority** - The belief, based on the naturalistic concept of the priority of the collective, that concentrated political power

that governmental power ought to be decentralized.	most effectively promotes the survival of social groupings.
Separation of powers - The belief that political power ought to be limited, based on the biblical concept that human beings are naturally sinful and corrupt, and that concentrated power allows the moral weakness of man to take advantage of the population at large.	**Concentration of power** - The belief that centralized political power is best able to promote the survival of society, based on the naturalistic concept that the collective has priority over the individual.

Worldview Beliefs Necessary for a Democratic Republic to Effectively Work

A democratic republic is one that is administered by politicians, but run by the citizens. That is to say that while the citizens are actually the ones who are ultimately in charge, nonetheless they elect representatives to stand in for them to take care of the actual work of governing.

The model that exists in America was established based on the biblical concept of stewardship. A steward is one who works for another in a managerial position and is responsible for carrying out the desires of the owner. In a very real way, politicians are stewards of the positions they occupy and are responsible to the citizens who elect them.

In the case of the American republic, though, there is another level of stewardship. The citizens are also stewards with responsibility to oversee the elected politicians on behalf of their owner – God. As such, citizens have a stewardship responsibility to elect people who will carry out the purposes of God in the world, and to keep an eye on them to make sure they are doing it well. If not, they need to be removed from office so a more faithful person can be selected. It is for this reason that voting is so important.

But in our current societal situation, here in America, not everyone believes in a biblical worldview understanding of governing. Those who are Naturalists do not even recognize God, nor do they follow a stewardship model of governing. Naturalism has no other choice but to operate by the law of the jungle. Those who are able to gain power get to make the rules, and the citizens must be forced to obey.

Let's take a moment now to more fully contrast the approach and values of these two conflicting worldview beliefs. During election seasons, citizens tend to pay more attention to the various issues that relate to the governing of our nation. Of course, these issues are continually before us, not just during campaign periods. However, it is during these times that the citizenry has the opportunity to select representatives who will promote the kinds of policies that correspond to what they believe. Thus, they tend to pay more attention.

In the heat of a campaign, people often get caught up in personalities and lose sight of the big picture issues. The candidates who are best able to resonate with the public, both by their words and their personality, are generally the ones people gravitate toward. But we must be careful at this point. While words and personality are important, what is far more important are principles and character.

We now live in a world that is dominated by a naturalistic worldview. As such, the principles that are most prominent in the public square tend to be based on naturalistic beliefs and values. And the people who dominate most of society's institutions tend to be people whose character is shaped by naturalistic principles. As Christians, we are called to a higher moral standard than the naturalist's law of the jungle – one that includes integrity, honesty, and selflessness. If we are truly guided by our faith, it is biblical principles that will guide our thoughts and actions, and which will shape our character.

Biblical Vs. Naturalistic Values

America was founded upon principles that emerged out of biblical beliefs. We are going to take a few moments now to take a deeper look at some of those principles and compare them to the naturalistic beliefs that currently challenge the traditional approach, and indeed shape the very landscape of American society.

The following is an explanation of some of these biblical principles and how they contrast with naturalistic ones.

Binding Vs. Non-Binding Foundation

<u>*Biblical View – Binding Foundation*</u>

There is a law that exists above human law – the law of God. This is not merely a set of suggested moral values, it is a revelation of the very character of God Himself, and of the actual structure of reality. God has not merely given us a list of rules to follow, He has revealed to us what His character is like and has commanded us to imitate Him. His character defines objectively real morality.

In revealing this knowledge to us, God gave it in the form of moral expectations. As such, it can be written as a set of rules and laws (for instance, see The Ten Commandments). However, it must be kept in mind, that merely keeping laws is not what pleases God. What He desires is that we become like Him.

Legalistically keeping the law is not sufficient because it is quite possible to keep the law outwardly yet have inner desires and motivations that contradict what is being outwardly expressed. When this happens, rules take priority over persons. That is simply not God's way. What God desires is people who lovingly and willingly live by His moral guidelines.

So, what we have is a foundational revelation that is unchanging based on the unchanging character of God. Human beings are called on by God to take that foundation and express it individually as they live daily life.

In American society, this concept has been taken as an organizing principle for our legal system. Our founders created a Constitution that was designed to be an unchanging foundation upon which all other laws would be based. Of course, being a human document, this Constitution is not unchangeable in the same way as

God's character. It can be changed, but based only on rules stated within the Constitution itself. It also cannot be interpreted differently from what was originally intended. (Psalm 1:1, 112:1-3; Proverbs 28:1-28; Ezekiel 36:27; Matthew 5:17-19; John 15:10; Romans 3:31; Galatians 3:21; 1 John 2:4)

Naturalistic View – Non-Binding Foundation

A naturalistic worldview does not acknowledge any sort of transcendent reality. As such, there is no one in existence who could possibly reveal a set of laws or rules that could be considered absolute and unchangeable.

Thus, in creating a legal foundation, those who hold to this worldview position do not see any compelling reason to look at the Constitution as an unchanging document. Rather, they see it as a "living and breathing" document that can be reinterpreted at any point by those who are in a position to do so (such as justices in the judicial system).

Civil Disobedience Vs. Strict Obedience to the Law

Biblical View – Civil Disobedience (Focus on the Individual)

The concept of civil disobedience is based squarely upon the presumption that there is a higher law than the temporal law of human society. The Bible clearly teaches that human beings ought to obey human law, and that promoting order in society is an essential part of God's will for mankind. That said, when civil law conflicts with God's revealed law in ways that prevent people from being obedient to God, His revelation is clear that the human law is illegitimate.

In that case, obedience to God is always the proper response. This very well may mean that an individual will receive punishment from the human authorities as a result of this disobedience. But allegiance to God is the Bible's ultimate standard for every human being. Any law that forces people to disobey God is illegitimate and is not to be obeyed. (Exodus 1:15-22; Daniel 3:1-30; Acts 4:18-20, 5:28-29; Romans 13:1-10)

Naturalistic View – Strict Obedience to the Rulers (Focus on the Collective)

In Naturalism, there is no higher law than that which is established by the governing authorities. As such, civil disobedience is recognized as illegitimate and cannot be not tolerated. There must be strict adherence to the commands of the ruling authorities so as to maintain order in society.

High Vs. Low Value of Individual Human Life

Biblical View – High Value of Human Life

Based on a biblical worldview, human beings are persons specially created in the image of God. We have a spiritual existence and spiritual qualities that are of a different order than other created creatures. Human beings have a capacity to participate in an objectively real personal relationship with God that is not possible for any other material creatures.

Because of this special status, those who follow biblical beliefs have a high view of human life. The Bible teaches that no one is allowed to take innocent human life, and to do so is a particular offense against God. As such, all laws and rules that humans create should have a built-in bias toward not killing innocent human life by any means. (Genesis 1:27; Deuteronomy 27:25; Jeremiah 1:5; Luke 12:42-46)

Naturalistic View – Low Value of Human Life

Based on a naturalistic worldview, human beings are merely one form of natural animal that is no more special than any other natural animal in existence. Human beings are recognized to have unique characteristics based upon their larger and more complex brain, but this uniqueness does not, in any way, provide special status to the human animal. In fact, other animals are seen to be actually superior in other ways (ex. faster, stronger, more stealthy, etc.). Thus, all animals are understood to be equally valuable in an objective sense.

Naturalistic belief asserts that every life form arrived at its current state based on naturalistic evolution. With that as a starting premise, all living things are merely part of an evolutionary continuum. That being the case, human life has no more intrinsic value than any other life form.

With that kind of reasoning, such things as abortion, euthanasia, capital punishment, or any other form of taking life, is not viewed as a bad thing in and of itself. It can only be good or bad based on the particular circumstances surrounding it. If it is deemed by society (or those who hold political power) to be good for the survival of the collective, there is no moral wrong to be considered. So, when societal laws and rules are created, the life of any particular individual is secondary to what is considered to be the needs of the collective.

Equality of Opportunity Vs. Equality of Outcomes

Biblical View – Equality of Opportunity (Focus on the Individual)

The concept of equality can be expressed in various ways. Based on biblical worldview beliefs, equality is based on the value of the individual. God has created individuals with special value and with unique abilities. In order to achieve excellence and accomplish God's purpose for their lives, the Bible teaches that each person is to be a good steward of those gifts by using them as effectively as they can in life.

Not everyone is the same. Different people were created with abilities to excel in different areas of life. As a result, the outcomes of people's efforts will be different based on their personal decisions and strengths.

The biblical revelation expresses the idea that individuals should be provided with the freedom to pursue their lives based on their gifting from God. This promotes the idea that everything everyone does in response to God's leading is of value. As such, everyone ought to be provided with an equal opportunity in life to pursue this leading from God. (Proverbs 22:2; Matthew 5:43-48; Romans 10:12; James 2:1-4)

Naturalistic View – Equality of Outcome (Focus on the Collective)

A naturalistic worldview is based on a completely different set of underlying values than biblical values. Rather than valuing the special gifting of individuals, the focus of Naturalism is on promoting the survival and advancement of the collective. As such, individuals are encouraged to pursue their own opportunities only to the degree that it promotes the higher value of the collective.

In cases where it is deemed by those who control society that certain needs must be accounted for, the opportunity of individuals to pursue their own desires can be legitimately curtailed.

Individual Vs. Collective Liberty

Biblical View – Individual Liberty (Focus on the Individual & Freedom of Conscience)

Based on a biblical worldview, the individual has priority over the collective. As such, all laws and societal rules should be crafted in such a way as to promote the growth and development of individuals. This does not mean that the collective should not be taken into account, only that the individual is the most important consideration. It is society's duty to create an environment that facilitates and encourages an individual's willingness and ability to move into arenas that benefit society. Still, the final decision must be left to the individual.

The reason for a priority on the individual is that God created individual human beings for the specific purpose of relationship with Himself. To pursue this, each person must have the freedom to make decisions that move them in that direction. God created mankind with that ability and revealed that all should live life based on that principle. (Deuteronomy 24:16; Proverbs 9:12; Isaiah

61:1-11; Jeremiah 31:30, 34:8, 15-17; Ezekiel 18:20; John 8:36; Romans 13:1-10; 2 Corinthians 3:17, 5:10; Galatians 5:1, 13; James 1:25)

Naturalistic View – Collective Liberty (Priority of and Focus on the Collective)

A naturalistic worldview, on the other hand, is based on a belief that the highest value is the survival of the species. Since it does not acknowledge the existence of God, and it views human beings as nothing more than one part of an evolved natural order, individuals are only valuable as they contribute to the survival of the collective. Thus, if those who are in a position to make society's rules judge that the collective would be better served by allowing either the harming or promotion of certain individuals or classes of individuals, that could be deemed acceptable.

Impartial Vs. Partial Judges

Biblical View – Impartial Judges

The idea of impartiality, as it relates to the legal system, seems only fair to most people. However, the very concept of fairness, itself, must be based on some overarching principle. Based on biblical teachings, that would be the revelation of God Himself. As such, fairness, as expressed in the Bible, becomes an absolute that cannot be violated. The Bible teaches that God, Himself, is impartial in his judgment of mankind, and has revealed that this is a point of view that should characterize human judgment of other humans. (Leviticus 19:1, 15, 35-37; Deuteronomy 1:16-17; Proverbs 11:1, 16:10-13)

Naturalistic View – Partial Judges (The Greater Good)

Naturalism has no absolute moral base. Since a naturalistic point of view asserts that the natural universe is all that exists, the most important principle for society can only take into account material reality. As it relates to humanity, it is most essential to promote human survival by emphasizing the greater good of the collective. This may include impartiality in making judgments, but even that is not an absolute. A naturalistic approach could just as easily allow for partiality if the judge believes that would be better for the greater good of the collective. There is nothing in Naturalism that demands fairness.

Due Process Vs. Arbitrary Process

Biblical View – Due Process

Due process is another expression of a biblical worldview based on God's revelation. This principle refers to the necessity of having the opportunity for an individual to tell his or her side of the story during any judicial proceeding. The idea is that one cannot be deprived of life, liberty, or individual stewardship responsibility, unless this qualification has been met. Once again, this is seen as an absolute principle. The Bible conveys the idea that due process is an expression of the kind of fairness and justice that God exhibits, and that He expects society to follow. (Deuteronomy 25:1-3, 19:15; Numbers 35:30)

Naturalistic View – Arbitrary Process (The Greater Good)

Based on a naturalistic worldview, proper due process is not necessarily a bad thing, but it is also not absolute. For something to be absolute, there must be some absolute basis for its existence, and since Naturalism has no foundation for absolute values, it is understood that there may be times when due process is not in the best interest of the collective. The more appropriate standard in Naturalism would be the interests of the collective – which is determined by those who hold power in the society.

Equal Vs. Arbitrary Justice Under the Law

Biblical View – Equal Justice Under the Law

Another expression of a biblical worldview is equal justice under the law. This is the belief that everyone, no matter their station in life, is of equal value, and that justice should not be portioned out based on an individual's life circumstance. In this view, the law, rather than human status, is the ultimate basis for judgment. The very idea of equal justice under that law is based on the belief that God, Himself, judges this way, and has revealed that human beings should judge likewise in their legal system. (Deuteronomy 16:18; 2 Chronicles 19:7; Ephesians 6:9)

Naturalistic View – Arbitrary Justice (The Greater Good)

Once again, Naturalists don't necessarily dismiss the concept of equal justice under the law out of hand. Many, if not most, would probably recognize this, generally, as a good basis for judicial practice. That said, there is nothing to establish it as an absolute standard. It is those who are judging who must set the ultimate standard, as Naturalists do not acknowledge any source for a transcendent law. Thus, if those who hold power perceive that equal justice, in particular circumstances, does not further the greater good of the collective, a different standard can be used.

Formal Vs. Arbitrary Accusations

Biblical View – Formal Accusations

The purpose for requiring formal accusations is to promote justice based on truth, rather than on the personal desires of those who hold power. It is quite easy for an individual to accuse another of wrongdoing out of a desire for personal gain. A formal accusation establishes a framework whereby the person being accused has the ability to understand the accusation, as well as the opportunity to respond.

Once again, this principle is an expression of biblical revelation. Based on biblical teachings, human beings have the ability to freely choose to do right or wrong. Choosing against God is the very definition of sin and is that which separates a person from Him. To get that problem corrected, individuals must understand their sin so they can repent.

God, in His revelation, has explained to humanity what sin looks like and why it is an offense against Him. The revelation, then, becomes a formal accusation to which the individual is able to respond. This principle is held forth as one that expresses a proper element of justice in the legal process. (Deuteronomy 17:6, 19:15; Matthew 18:16; 1 Timothy 5:19)

Naturalistic View – Arbitrary Accusations (The Greater Good)

As with previous principles, the naturalistic belief about formal accusations is based upon a naturalistic worldview. And as before, Naturalists don't necessarily see providing formal accusations to be a bad thing – it is just not absolute. At those times when the "powers that be" believe that providing formal accusations may not be in the best interest of the collective, there is no compelling reason to operate on that basis. The most compelling standard in Naturalism remains the greater good of the collective – which is determined by those who hold power in society.

Legal Vs. Arbitrary Rules in Trials

Biblical View – Legal Rules in Trials

The purpose of a legal trial is to provide the person being accused of a crime a means to be fairly treated based on true justice, rather than on the capriciousness of those in power. A legal trial is one that is conducted based on a standard set of rules that cannot be violated. No individual, or group, should have the power to accuse or convict a person of a crime based on arbitrary rules, or on their own authority.

As before, this principle is an expression of biblical revelation. When God judges human beings for their sin, it is not done in an arbitrary manner. The rules of judgment are firmly established based on a fixed, and known, set of spiritual laws that God has revealed to mankind. God impartially judges humanity based on these unchanging principles. He has revealed that human society should also operate using this principle. (Deuteronomy 1:16, 17:9; Exodus 18:21-22)

Naturalistic View – Arbitrary Rules in Trials (The Greater Good)

While many, if not most, Naturalists would agree that having "legal trials" is a good, and even proper, standard, Naturalism does not provide a basis for making that judgment. In Naturalism, there is no absolute standard for any moral claim, as there is no authority that can be considered absolute. All moral expressions must be created and judged by those in society who have the power or authority to do so. Legal trials can be seen as good in circumstances where it helps maintain order in society. But if there are deemed to be circumstances where it is considered that the greater good of the collective is served by shifting to a different set of rules, there is no reason why that can't be done, as well.

Conclusion – The Foundation of Values Matters

In American society, biblical worldview beliefs are, without question, the basis for understanding right morality and fairness – in the legal system and throughout the rest of society. Even those who are not Christians generally acknowledge the "rightness" of these beliefs.

That said, when the source for the beliefs is denigrated or set aside, it will not be very long before the beliefs themselves erode. Even when the beliefs are considered to be a proper ideal, when the foundation for the beliefs is not understood to be absolute, they may be put aside in circumstances where it is considered to benefit the "greater good of the collective" (based on the evaluation of those who hold power).

The source of values matters. There is a way reality is actually structured. God does exist and has spoken to mankind in His revelation. In that revelation, He has given us guidance as to what is right and wrong, and we do not have a right to alter it.

To the degree we acknowledge God and follow His ways, we will thrive – individually and as a society. To the degree we push Him aside, we will collapse into ruin.

Values Necessary for a Democratic Republic to Work Effectively and Thrive

I n order for a Democratic Republic to work effectively, it is necessary for certain values, moral principles, and/or core beliefs to be commonly agreed upon. If values such as the following are not the ones governing society, a Democratic Republic is virtually impossible to maintain. Those values include life, liberty, pursuit of happiness (property rights), moral purity, justice, and love.

There are those, of course, who would object to this assertion and insist that a different value set could dominate and a democratic republic would still work. In particular, those who hold a naturalistic worldview try to make that argument. They assert that the only thing necessary is an agreed upon social contract that includes the necessary elements for it to work. In spite of that objection, however, a social contract alone simply will not work.

The reason it won't work is that Naturalism can't provide a commonly agreed upon objective authority source that can be depended upon. In fact, the very notion of a social contract capable of governing the values of society goes against human nature itself. There will always be people who want to step into positions of power who are willing to not only break the social contract, but force an entirely new set of values on the citizenry that suits their preferences – and, for them, there is no objective reason why the new values are not just as valid as the old.

In truth, the values necessary for a democratic republic to work are specifically based on the values of Christian

Theism. They are derived from an understanding that these values are objectively true and real because they are based on the character of an unchanging, objectively real personal God who has revealed them to mankind.

In order to grasp the religious nature of the values we are dealing with, we need a way of identifying the religious foundation of the beliefs. We do this by answering three simple questions:

> 1. What is the nature of ultimate reality? (Who is God?)
>
> 2. What is a human being? (What is man?)
>
> 3. What is the ultimate a person can get out of life? (What is salvation?)

Understanding Christian Theistic Belief

Christian Theism answers these three questions in a particular way.

> 1. There exists an eternal God who created the natural universe out of nothing. This God is the one who is revealed in the Bible.
>
> 2. Human beings are persons created in the image of God but are fallen.

3. The ultimate a person can get out of life is to enter into an eternal personal relationship with God based on the atoning death and resurrection of Jesus Christ.

The Nature of Christian Theistic Belief

The most basic element of Christian Theism relates to the fact that it is personal. God has revealed that He Himself is a single personal being who exists as a Trinitarian person (three persons in one eternal being). Without spending an enormous amount of time trying to explain the Trinity, it is sufficient here to simply note that the essential existence of this Trinitarian God is relational as the three persons in the Trinity relate personally to one another in their eternal environment.

When God created human beings, He did not create other Trinitarian beings, but He did make man in His image in the sense that He created humans as persons with all of the essential elements of personhood. With that as a starting point, the existence of personal relationships become the most central element of human existence. God made man capable of engaging in a personal relationship with Himself and with other human persons. And it is this characteristic that forms the basis for the belief that the individual has priority over the collective.

So, what about the moral values Christian Theism promotes? It promotes a type of morality that values the individual above the collective, and it puts individuals in a position to accomplish the purpose of God in their human life in the here and now.

Understanding Naturalistic Belief

Naturalism also has its own unique way that it answers the three essential belief questions:

> 1. The natural universe, operating by natural laws, is all that exists.
>
> 2. Human beings are purely material animals that naturally evolved to their current place in the evolutionary chain.
>
> 3. The ultimate a person can get out of life is to physically survive, and personally decide upon, and achieve, personal fulfillment.

The Nature of Naturalistic Belief

If you look carefully at the three answers Naturalism gives, you can't help but notice that all of them are faith assumptions. There is not a single one that can be demonstrated using scientific discovery. This is quite revealing, as the most basic assumption of a naturalistic worldview is that the natural universe is all that exists. If that is true, then it also has to be true that everything is explainable based on the natural laws of the universe, and that science can ultimately discover how everything, without exception, works.

So how is it that NOTHING Naturalists assert in answer to these three questions can be explained by science? While the belief system requires that science be able to answer them (as there is no other possibility), the most foundational beliefs of the system are not based on science at all – they are based on faith.

Beyond that, what about the moral values Naturalism promotes? The beliefs that form the basis for Naturalism are based purely on the personal preferences of those who make the laws of society. And that is the biggest problem with Naturalism as it relates to naturalistic morality.

The bottom line of this belief system is power – the ones with the power get to decide the moral values everyone else must live by. They do not acknowledge the existence of any transcendent or absolutely objective values. Since they don't believe there is any such thing as objective "Truth," they have no choice but to make it up for themselves – and they must do so based on their own personal preferences.

How Values are Expressed in Naturalism and Christian Theism

Life

The right to life is the most basic human right. Based on a biblical worldview, this right is not limited to certain groups or classes of humans; it is sacrosanct. The biblical approach to this is that no one has the right to take innocent human life. There are situations where taking a life is legitimate, but never when it comes to "innocent" human life.

Based on Christian Theism, human life is considered sacred because it is created by God. Beyond that, the Bible teaches that human beings are created in the image of God, specifically for the purpose of a personal relationship with Him. And, as already mentioned, the Bible also clearly teaches that it is immoral to take innocent human life.

Naturalists, though, have an entirely different understanding. Based on naturalistic beliefs, humans are nothing more than one species of natural animal among many. A human is born, lives its natural life, and dies – the end.

In naturalistic philosophy, life is definitely considered important, but not the life of any particular individual.

Rather, the focus is on the collective; it is the survival of the collective that is critical, not any particular individual. This focus on the collective is widely expressed as "the survival of the species."

Since the collective, rather than the individual, is what is important, what happens to particular individuals takes a secondary position. Thus, if any given individual's life is not considered helpful for the advancement of society in general, it is not a problem to remove the offending individual. As such, when society's leaders consider that there are too many babies being born, or if having a baby creates problems for the collective, then abortion is considered a perfectly acceptable practice. The exact same principle applies as it relates to the elderly or to those who have various physical or mental disabilities. It is acceptable to terminate their lives if it becomes too much of a burden on society.

Similarly, if it is deemed that the population of the planet is getting too large, it is acceptable for the ruling authorities to take measures to decrease the population – by whatever means necessary. There is no other necessary moral consideration.

Liberty

In July of 2016, a group of four preachers, two British and two American, were doing some open air preaching outside of a shopping center in Bristol, England. In their preaching, they asserted that the only way to come to God was through Jesus Christ. They also enumerated a number of sins that would keep people away from God.

As they preached, some of the people who heard them were offended and called a police officer who ordered the preachers to leave the area. He told them that they were not welcome, and were causing a disturbance. When the men would not leave, the officer arrested them.

Later, charges were dropped for two of the preachers. The other two, however, went to trial and were convicted of "intentionally alarming the public with their preaching." The prosecutor, Ian Jackson, issued a press release where he stated, "To say to someone that Jesus is the only God is not a matter of truth. To the extent that they are saying that the only way to God is through Jesus, that cannot be a truth." He also said that it was wrong for the preachers to include homosexuals in a list of sinners, and that doing so must be considered to be abusive and a criminal matter.

In the end, those two preachers were convicted of violating Britain's Crime and Disorder Act that prohibits speech or behavior causing intentional harassment, alarm, or distress that is racially or religiously aggravated. They were fined about $2,500.00 each.

It is amazing that something like this could happen in the UK, but similar things are happening in America, as well. Barronelle Stutzman, a florist in Washington state, was convicted in court of discrimination because she turned down a job to create floral arrangements for a gay wedding. A similar thing happened to the owners of Sweet Cakes By Melissa when the Oregon Bureau of Labor and Industry ordered the owners to bake a cake for a lesbian wedding. When they declined, the state forced them to pay $135,000.00 in damages to the lesbian couple they turned away.

And in Wisconsin, there is a law that says creative professionals must be willing to promote messages that violate their religious beliefs. Under that law, photographer Amy Lawson is barred from turning down business that would force her to promote pro-abortion causes or gay marriage. Those who violate the state law are subject to severe criminal fines of up to $10,000.00, business license suspension or revocation, as well as civil and punitive damages.

To traditional American sensibilities, these limitations on freedom seem rather outrageous, but this kind of thing is becoming increasingly common. Why is it happening? The answer has to do with the religious beliefs these laws are based upon.

To be sure, the people who create these kinds of laws, and those who prosecute them, do not see any religious element to them. In these people's minds, the laws are purely secular – without any religious content whatsoever. In their thinking, they are simply preventing discrimination.

However, nothing could be further from the truth. The fact is, they are not preventing discrimination at all. Rather, they are actually legalizing discrimination against those who disagree with their religious viewpoint.

While adherents of these kinds of laws truly believe that their directives are religiously neutral, they are not! In fact, they are immanently religious in nature. The very basis of all these kinds of laws is spawned from naturalistic worldview beliefs.

How These Beliefs Are Applied to Make Law

When it comes to making laws based on naturalistic beliefs, we need to understand that they must be created based on the personal preferences of the ones designing and enforcing them. Since Naturalists acknowledge no transcendent law giver, there is no other possibility. With that as a starting point, there cannot be any law or moral value that is universally right. People have to make it up for themselves as they go along.

So here is how that works:

For whatever reason, the ones in power decide on a definition of discrimination, arbitrarily deem it to be immoral, then selectively apply the definition to the classes of behavior that they want to discourage or eliminate. The result is that they end up supporting one set of people as aggrieved while sanctioning all those who disagree with their definition. For instance, when the florist in Washington was convicted of discriminating against a homosexual customer, the court, by default, also decided that discriminating against the beliefs of the florist was okay. Since Naturalism recognizes no objective foundation for values, the basis for the court's decision was necessarily the personal preferences and opinions of the government officials.

Interestingly, those who prosecute these cases do not see the selectivity of their preferences. They really do believe that they are deciding rightly – even objectively. This speaks to the unconscious nature of worldview beliefs. Worldview beliefs are, for most people, so foundational that they are not even aware of them. They are based upon what particular individuals understand to be real and not real.

Thus, if an offender's beliefs are not considered by the authorities to represent reality while their own beliefs are seen to be real, then they consider that the outcome should be obvious to all. The only problem is, while they deem their beliefs to be objective truth, in actuality they are not – they are merely beliefs.

The End Result is the Destruction of Liberty

So, what is the end result of this kind of thinking? Beliefs that do not correspond to the preferences of the powerful are deemed crimes. What is right and wrong, legal and illegal, is based upon people's personal preferences, so any act that runs contrary to those preferences can be deemed a crime – and that is exactly what has happened in the illustrations above. Not making flower arrangements or not baking a cake for a homosexual wedding was considered criminal discrimination. Not taking a job photographing a pro-abortion rally can be considered criminal discrimination. When this kind of mindset is the basis of law and morality, freedom of conscience is set aside, and individual civil rights trampled on.

A naturalistic worldview basis for law and morality puts the personal preferences of the powerful above the conscience rights of the individual. As a result, the only people who are free to think and act according to their own beliefs are those who agree with those in power. Everyone else must, by necessity, give up their beliefs or face sanctions.

True liberty requires a belief in absolutes and a respect for the rights of conscience. A naturalistic basis for creating law will only result in tyranny. It is only biblical beliefs that are able to provide an objective basis for liberty of conscience.

The True Nature of Liberty

The beliefs of Christian Theism concerning liberty are based on the belief that mankind was created with free will. God's purpose for giving this attribute to humanity is based on His purpose for creating mankind in the first place – for personal fellowship with Himself. In order for there to be an actual relationship, both parties must be able to freely choose to engage one another. Individual liberty is the core of that possibility. It is this characteristic of mankind that is at the root of why American values promote liberty.

When it comes to a naturalistic worldview environment, however, individual liberty is not an important value. In fact, it is often seen as a detriment to the smooth operation of society. Once again, the idea that the collective takes priority over the individual is the key principle that informs the Naturalist's thinking about liberty.

In a society dominated by naturalistic beliefs, someone (or group) must decide what a smoothly operating society looks like. When that is determined, those who don't agree are seen to be harmful to the collective and must be suppressed. Individuals are free to do as they like as long as their actions conform to society's smooth operation (the survival of the species) based upon the dictates of those who hold power.

In a very profound way, liberty applies to virtually every area of life. When we look at the Constitution of the United States, we see a complete bias toward individual liberty and the exclusion of a collectivist approach to organizing society. Perhaps one of the most obvious examples of this is seen in the first amendment to the U.S. Constitution.

It guarantees the individual freedom of religion, freedom of speech, freedom of the press, freedom of peaceful assembly, and the freedom for individuals to petition the government over grievances. All of these, without exception, are guarantees designed to protect individual liberty. They are the promotion of a value system that is contrary to a collectivist approach to rights that restrict individual liberty.

Pursuit of Happiness

The American Declaration of Independence lists life, liberty, and the pursuit of happiness as inalienable human rights given to mankind by God. The implication is that human beings do not have the right to infringe on other people's lives in these categories. The concepts of life and liberty are fairly easy to grasp in this regard, and we have already looked at them above. The pursuit of happiness, on the other hand, tends not to be as well understood by most people. As it turns out, the English language has changed over the years, and the modern meaning of this phrase doesn't reflect a full understanding of what was meant when it was inserted into the Declaration of Independence.

In modern times, happiness is mostly associated with a person's personal sense of pleasure and well-being. Back when the document was written, however, it had a broader meaning. It carried the sense of prosperity or well-being. It was not merely the right to chase one's dreams, but additionally the right to do what one needed to do to "accomplish" prosperity and well-being. It was a call for the government not to interfere with people's property and livelihood in ways that would prevent them from accomplishing what they were going after in life.

In American society today there is a massive culture war going on. Just to be clear, a culture war can possibly be expressed in outward acts of discrimination and even violence; but make no mistake, its root is not discrimination or violence – it is ideology. And the ideological clash in modern America is a clash between Christian Theism and Naturalism.

When put in terms of ideology, many people immediately think that we are talking about matters related to politics. Of course, there will be political (as well as economic, moral, legal, and other) expressions. But in its essence, ideology is not a material category – it is spiritual. The culture war expressions are actually a clash of values between two opposing religions. There are many people who would chafe at this characterization, as they don't consider themselves religious. However, the characterization is absolutely true.

Some of the more common outward expressions of this war being played out in America today include such things as:

- The war against the police,

- The fight over abortion,

- The fight over control of health care,

- Attempts to limit free speech on college campuses and other places,

- The fight about "separation of church and state,"

- The dispute over the meaning of marriage,

- The battle over various attempts at wealth redistribution,

- The battle over critical race theory in public education,

- The dispute over transgender rights and for minors to transition to a different sex,

- The use of force and violence to accomplish political ends in protest marches and other places.

While the culture war is, at its core, a spiritual war, the most prominent outward expressions tend to be political. The traditional American political expression based on Christian Theism involves the promotion of individual liberty. Here, the concept of the pursuit of happiness comes to the forefront based on the notion that the government should not do things that limit an individual's ability to accomplish his or her life goals.

The other side of the conflict in this war is based on Naturalism and expresses itself in political terms that promote various forms of collectivism (Socialism, Communism, and the like). Based on this point of view, the pursuit of happiness trends not toward limiting government's influence over the individual, but toward using the government as an instrument to accomplish things within the collective to make people's lives easier. Of course, it is those in positions of power and influence who get to decide what that should be.

With an understanding of the beliefs of Christian Theism and Naturalism, it becomes possible to see how that plays out regarding the Pursuit of Happiness. In Christian Theism, God is recognized as the owner of the entirety of His creation. However, He has also chosen mankind to partner with Him to accomplish His purpose in the world.

In doing this, He has appointed humans to serve as stewards (managers) of the world He made. As stewards, individual humans are given various forms of property to manage for God. It is this principle of stewardship that is behind the American value of private property ownership and free market expression.

Based on the beliefs of Naturalism, the entirety of reality can be explained by the natural laws of the universe – which gives Naturalism an entirely different way of evaluating the meaning of the pursuit of happiness. It begins with the belief that the ultimate in life is survival, so the collective has a higher value than the individual. With that as a starting point, a socialist/communist (or some other totalitarian) approach to life naturally emerges as the best means to protect and provide for the collective. As it relates to the pursuit of happiness, it is only natural that property, and the means of production, be owned, or at least controlled, by the state. It is considered that a central authority is best able to coordinate the production and supply of goods and services in a way that promotes the welfare (thus the happiness) of the collective.

Moral Purity

Based on the most common ways of viewing religious expression, Sweden is considered the least religious nation in the world. (Of course, that is not true based on a worldview perspective, as their religious foundation is actually Naturalism. They are just as religiously active in their faith as anyone who follows any other religion.) Sociologist Phil Zuckerman spent 14 months interviewing people in Sweden to try and understand their view of God. His findings: People are not so much anti-God as they are utterly oblivious to religious matters. Eighty percent of the population consider themselves either "not religious" or "convinced atheists."

Sweden is not the only country, though, that can be considered "non-religious." In 2012, Toronto, Canada passed a "transgender law" that made "schools legally responsible for eliminating barriers to inclusion based on gender identity and gender expression." So, what has been the result of this new law? Recently, a Toronto public school teacher announced he would use "all-gender cabins" for students on school camping trips. In making the decision to do this, because of the law, the school did not even need to obtain parental permission.

Beyond that, this teacher declared that "wearing underwear around the cabin was acceptable for boys and girls, and for those who identify as 'boy' or 'girl.'" The teacher played down the possibility of sexual activity among the children, stating that the students had been taught to "sensitively articulate both the policies in place prohibiting the behavior and the underlying heteronormativity of the concern." In other words, the kids had been taught that looking at or thinking about another person in a sexual way based on their biological gender was wrong. Because of this instruction, the teacher was convinced they would not act out.

Of course, what is not overtly stated, but is implied in the teacher's statement, is that the only sin in that situation was thinking of sex in terms of biological gender. If a student's reason for thinking and acting sexually was not based on biological gender, there was nothing improper. You see, the "transgender law" is not just about people who self-identify as transgendered. It is a subterfuge to change the very basis for understanding what moral and immoral sexual behavior actually entails.

But that is Sweden and Canada. It is unimaginable that, with America's biblical heritage, we would ever arrive at a place where God is simply a non-factor as in those countries, right? Sadly, both of these examples illustrate exactly where America is moving. The Sweden illustration demonstrates where we are going religiously and philosophically, while the Canada example expresses how that belief gets expressed in society. And just a note, both of those countries used to be dominated by Christian values.

A large swath of American society has already become Sweden. It is not difficult at all to find videos of roving reporters on social media asking people about their belief in God and getting the same kinds of answers the pollsters got in Sweden. By the same token, we see articles in newspapers and magazines virtually every day reporting on efforts being made to pass the very same transgender laws that Toronto is using to promote sexual deviance among their children.

While all of America has not yet moved to the level of Sweden and Canada, it is evident that we are rapidly shifting in that direction. One of the indications of that happening is what is evident in a certain segment of the so called "Christian" population. Sadly, the worldview beliefs behind the anti-God movement in secular society are finding their way into many churches, as well.

We see it in denominations that follow forms of theology that deny the core beliefs of the Christian faith. The people associated with these groups and theological positions self-identify as Christians, and even keep the facade of the church. However, they have adopted a belief system that substitutes social justice (temporal salvation) for the biblical teachings about the true nature of sin and salvation.

One website that promotes "Progressive Christianity" (https://progressivechristianity.org), lists eight basic principles that characterize their beliefs. It states: By calling ourselves progressive Christians, we mean we are Christians who...

> 1. Believe that following the path and teachings of Jesus can lead to an awareness and experience of the Sacred and the Oneness and Unity of all life;

> 2. Affirm that the teachings of Jesus provide but one of many ways to experience the Sacredness and Oneness of life, and that we can draw from diverse sources of wisdom in our spiritual journey;

> 3. Seek community that is inclusive of ALL people, including but not limited to: conventional Christians and questioning skeptics, believers and agnostics, women and men, those of all sexual orientations and gender identities, and those of all classes and abilities;

4. Know that the way we behave towards one another is the fullest expression of what we believe;

5. Find grace in the search for understanding, and believe there is more value in questioning than in absolutes;

6. Strive for peace and justice among all people;

7. Strive to protect and restore the integrity of our Earth;

8. Commit to a path of life-long learning, compassion, and selfless love.

9. Other beliefs associated with "Progressive Christianity" include:

- An understanding of spirituality as a psychological or neural state;

- Critical interpretation of the scripture as a record of human historical and spiritual experiences, and theological reflection;

- Acceptance of people who have differing understandings of the concept of "God;" such as Pantheism, Deism, and Non-theism;

- An affirmation of both human spiritual unity and social diversity;

- A steadfast solidarity with the poor as the subjects of their own emancipation, rather than being the objects of charity;

- Compassion for all living beings.

If you read these statements carefully, you will see that the beliefs being promoted include Unitarianism, Universalism, acceptance of any lifestyle as moral, acceptance of any sincerely held belief as legitimate, economic and social equality as the basis for salvation, morality based on relativism, environmental and animal rights activism, and biblical interpretation based on naturalistic hermeneutic principles. What we have here is the creation of a theological statement that does not begin with biblical teachings; rather, it begins with naturalistic worldview presuppositions, then interprets the Bible through that filter. So, when it comes time to interpret the Bible, those who adhere to this belief cherry-pick passages out of context that support their beliefs and ignore anything that doesn't.

One common example we can point to that is a particularly strong emphasis of Progressive Christians relates to the belief that the purpose of Jesus' ministry on earth was to "fight for the poor and the down and out." Now, this does not sound so far-fetched ... until you dig a little deeper to see the true intention of that phrase. What is really being asserted is that salvation involves using political and economic pressure to change the balance of power in society to favor the poor over the more well off.

The mechanism for doing this is the redistribution of a nation's wealth. They do this by instituting Communist and Socialist principles. When this redistribution is accomplished, they believe justice has been achieved in society, and the people have been saved.

By reinterpreting the purpose of Jesus in this way, "Progressive Christians" literally take away the moral authority of God and the Bible. In its place, the authority source becomes their progressive principles – which are based purely on the opinions of those who hold this point of view. The result is, by taking away the focus on eternal salvation, all that is left is a focus on material circumstances – which is then bolstered by the various liberal theological positions.

We already mentioned a couple of places where this plays out in real life – changing the economic and political plight of the poor by force of law, for instance. But there are others, such as:

- the acceptance of beliefs that come from non-biblical sources;

- the acceptance and approval of all other religious traditions;

- salvation as an economic and political outcome (as opposed to spiritual regeneration);

- the use of liberal theological paradigms (as opposed to acceptance of the authority of the Bible);

- peace and justice as a purely material outcome, as opposed to a spiritual end;

- an emphasis on environmental and animal rights activism as a means of promoting justice;

- an understanding of spirituality as nothing more than a psychological or physiological state;

- the promotion of anti-establishment political activism and Socialism/Communism as the means of salvation.

What this Has to Do with Moral Purity

At this point, you may be wondering what all this has to do with the concept of moral purity. The answer is, there is a direct correlation between a person's beliefs and the moral expression of those beliefs. When the foundation that defines morality is eliminated, the need for a foundation doesn't simply go away. What results is that a new foundation is inserted to take the place of the old. And the new foundation that has emerged in Western societies is based on Naturalism.

As was noted before, Naturalism is the belief that the natural universe, operating by natural laws, is all that exists. That being the case, there is no God, thus no transcendent moral values. The only possibility at this point is for human beings to make up their own morality. And that is exactly what has happened.

Based on Naturalism, there is no place for human life to be deemed sacred. Human beings are merely one animal species among many. If it is considered by the majority that abortion, doctor assisted suicide, euthanasia, infanticide, or the extermination of any given group is best for the survival of the collective, then it can be deemed okay.

Based on Naturalism, lying, stealing, or doing anything else that advances one's personal goals can be considered moral. Since there is no God (thus no moral absolutes), the ultimate goal in life becomes personal satisfaction and the survival of the collective. Literally anything can be considered moral in the quest to accomplish these objectives.

Based on Naturalism, there is no reason for considering the traditional family as "right." Whatever grouping "feels right" or is accepted by society, can be recognized as legitimate. This can include homosexual marriage, polygamy, polyandry, or any other grouping one can imagine.

Based on Naturalism, there is no such thing as right and wrong sexual morality. There is no reason why any form of sexual relations, inside or outside of marriage, cannot be considered legitimate (fornication, adultery, homosexuality, polygamy, pedophilia, polyamory, bestiality, etc.).

Virtually all of the things that have been traditionally considered moral based on biblical values have been set aside, and a naturalistic (relativistic) value system has been put in its place. As a result, we see immorality normalized in the entertainment industry and in society at large; we see dishonesty and lack of integrity normalized among our businesspeople and politicians; we see lies and distortion of the truth as an everyday element in reporting by our news media; and we see those educating our children basing their teaching on a belief system that promotes the acceptance of all of the above, thus diluting our country's moral purity even further.

The Meaning of Moral Purity

Moral purity relates to that which is right. Many people look at Christian Theism and think this simply means following a set of rules that are written down in the Bible.

While the biblical beliefs about morality are written down in the Bible, the source of that morality is not the Bible; it is God Himself.

The Bible is not simply a rule book authored by men. Rather, it is an expression of the very thoughts and character of God that He has revealed to man. He revealed His character to particular individuals who, then, wrote down what was revealed so that those coming after them would have that knowledge.

This revelation is not simply a list of moral dos and don'ts, but is an expression of the actual nature of reality – what is real and not real. Those who act contrary to that revelation are not simply breaking rules, they are living life in ways that literally contradict the laws of reality. And the consequences of living that way have personal, psychological, social, and spiritual consequences that end up destroying people's lives.

For example, those who act sexually in ways that are opposed to what is taught in the Bible are not merely breaking sexual rules, they are acting in ways that are contrary to the way man was created to act. As such, the consequences are not found simply in physical results (though there may be those as well), but also in emotional, psychological, and spiritual outcomes.

Of course, illicit expressions of sexuality are not the only places where morally impure acts take place. It also includes such things as all forms of bigotry and discrimination based strictly on superficial outward factors such as race, gender, and age. It includes things like lying, cheating, stealing, killing, slander, enslavement, evil speech, and the like. Then there are personal matters of moral impurity such as selfishness, improper pride, coveting, hatred, judgmentalism, and things of that nature.

As mentioned before, it is not simply a matter of doing a bad thing here and there; moral impurity is a matter of "being" before it is a matter of "doing." People act out of who they are; they act badly because there is an internal moral impurity at work. The focus of Christian Theism is on knowing God in order to become the kind of person who reflects the character of God. The focus of Naturalism is to accomplish particular temporal outward outcomes.

The effective operation of a democratic republic requires an inner restraint that willingly obeys laws and acts in ways that reflect the actual structure of reality (the revealed moral purity of God). When a large percentage of the population come to the place where they are not willing to live this way, we begin to see both individual and societal break down. This literally destroys a democratic republic from the inside out – and that is what is happening in America today.

Justice

Justice has to do with administering law or some other authority source according to the principles of what is right and fair. If justice is not rightly implemented, there can be no fairness in society.

That said, not everyone agrees on how justice should be properly implemented. And, as you might guess, the primary conflicts we see in modern society relate to the differing ways Christian Theists and Naturalists approach this subject.

Christian Theists promote what might be considered "actual justice." This involves protecting the innocent and punishing the guilty based on an absolute legal standard that cannot be violated. It also includes the notion that every citizen should receive equal justice under the law.

A naturalistic approach to justice does not recognize an absolute legal standard. It often uses the expression "Social Justice" to define its standard. This thinking is based on a relativistic approach to defining what is acceptable and unacceptable. Then, it metes out punishment based on the preferences of those who are doing the judging. It is known more for favoring particular groups over others rather than asserting equal justice under the law

What Is the Social Justice Movement?

The Social Justice movement has become popular in some circles over the last several years as a moral expression for creating fairness and justice in society. Social Justice, however, is not built upon total impartiality, nor on equal justice under the law. Rather, those who promote this approach to defining morality have their own specific criteria for determining what is just and unjust. In modern society it typically relates to wealth distribution, personal activity, and social privileges.

The concept of Social Justice hasn't always had the meaning we see promoted in modern society. In previous time periods, it was simply a way of referring to an emphasis on taking care of the physical needs of those who were down and out. This notion has been prominent throughout the history of the Christian church, as Christians have felt a particular calling to help the poor, the widowed, those in prison, and the like. The use of the term itself dates back to the eighteenth century, though it wasn't until the middle of the nineteenth century that it began to be used in the way we see it in modern times.

Although the sense of the concept of Social Justice would seem to be a natural fit as an expression of the Christian faith, today the term has been appropriated by people who hold a naturalistic worldview and is used in a way that suits their purposes. With that, it has lost its genuinely biblical emphasis. What has happened is that the meaning of the term has been changed to reflect a Socialist or Communist ideology. This can sometimes be quite confusing since most of the people who promote this kind of ideology, and who use the term most often, generally claim to be Christians. However, the Christians who advocate for Social Justice in this way are primarily members of groups that use an approach to interpreting the Bible that does not reflect traditional biblical theology.

The confusion many people have in understanding why the modern Social Justice movement is not a biblical approach arises primarily because of the way ideas are expressed. Those who promote it generally use Christian vocabulary to express their views on Social Justice, but they redefine those words using naturalistic worldview definitions. Rather than basing their moral foundation on the absolute platform of biblical theology, they base it upon the relativism of Naturalism.

A great case in point is the sermon an American Episcopal bishop preached at the wedding of Prince Harry and Meghan Markle in England. (A transcript of this wedding message can be viewed at: https://www.npr.org/sections/thetwoway/2018/05/20/61 2798691/bishop-michael-currys-royal-wedding sermon-full-text-of-the-power-of-love.)

Bishop Michael Curry spoke of Jesus, but his view of Jesus is that he was only a man, not the incarnate God spoken of in the Bible. And though he spoke much of "love," his meaning did not relate to the sacrificial love of God in Christ who died as an atoning sacrifice for the sins of mankind, but of a type of preferential love God has for the physically down and out. His sermon simply did not express the biblical concepts about God and love that it probably appeared to do for the uninitiated masses.

While biblical Theism looks at rights and duties from the perspective of the individual, contemporary Social Justice thinking considers rights and duties to be derived from the collective – the various institutions of society. Rather than expecting individuals to take responsibility for their own lives, with society picking up some of the slack when people fall short, Social Justice ideology looks to societal institutions to be the primary source for taking care of people. In the political arena, this is expressed by promoting a system where the government provides benefits and services to the citizenry, as opposed to expecting people to take individual responsibility for their own lives. To pull this off, they advocate that those who are the productive in society should be forced to support "the downtrodden" by paying higher taxes. They also advocate for manipulating and regulating markets to ensure "fair distribution of wealth," and "equal opportunity."

One of the biggest problems, though, as it relates to the promotion of Social Justice, is its reliance on moral relativism. Social Justice advocates are not really advocates of equal justice, as truly equal justice cannot exist in their philosophy. Rather, they pick and choose the people or groups they consider to be on the receiving end of unjust treatment based on their own arbitrary preferences. Adding the word "Social" to the word justice clearly demonstrates that the objective of these advocates is not justice for all, but to provide certain social advantages to those they deem to have received injustice.

As such, people in society are not looked upon as individuals, but as a collection of various groups that are either advantaged or disadvantaged. The advantaged groups must be taken down a notch by taking their "privilege" from them (money, power, prestige, etc.), while the disadvantaged must be helped by using the privilege taken from the "advantaged" and giving it to the "disadvantaged." Some of the various groups Social Justice proponents advocate for include migrants, prisoners, the physically and developmentally disabled, various racial and ethnic groups, and so on.

One of the more recent incarnations of liberal theology is Liberation Theology. Liberation theology is a movement which believes that the teachings of Jesus Christ do not promote eternal truths. Rather, they advocate for the elimination of unjust economic, political, or social conditions. It teaches that the essence of salvation (the purpose of the Christian faith) is to help the poor in their suffering by helping them overcome the oppression of a society that keeps them down. Essentially, it is Marxist Communism dressed up in biblical vocabulary using redefined biblical words.

Additionally, Liberation Theology comes in different strains: There is Black Liberation Theology, Asian Liberation Theology, Feminist Liberation Theology, Native American Liberation Theology, and on and on. In each of these, the disadvantaged group is specifically defined, and the named oppressors of these disadvantaged ones must "give up their advantage" by transferring it to the "oppressed." Obviously, the Social Justice movement is not based on biblical beliefs. Biblical beliefs define salvation as the forgiveness of sin provided by the sacrificial death and the resurrection of Jesus Christ. It has an eternal focus as opposed to the temporal focus of Social Justice thinking.

It is, of course, very possible that when a particular injustice appears, it affects an identifiable group of people. But providing justice does not come from transferring advantage from one group to another. It comes when the system itself is changed in a way that provides true justice to every individual, no matter what group they belong to. Based on a biblical worldview, the bottom line is the individual. That is the only point of view that can ever provide true justice.

There is no doubt that Christians should help the down and out and advocate for justice and equality. Those are decidedly Christian values. And the truth is, while certainly not perfect, Christians, as a community, have done more to promote that outcome than any other group in the history of the world. That said, the concepts of justice and equality cannot be allowed to be coopted, by changing the meaning of words.

What's Wrong with Social Justice?

The idea of Social Justice, on the surface, seems like it ought to be a good thing. It seems to be advocating a notion that all people should have access to proper justice. But the truth is, that is not what it is all about.

In fact, Social Justice, based on the modern usage of the term, does not advance justice at all. It promotes injustice. It promotes advantage toward a preferred group to the disadvantage of another. Christians should, in fact, be very concerned that true justice prevail in society. When we see injustice, we should point it out and make whatever changes need to be made to eliminate it.

Based on the ideas used to define Social Justice in modern society, it is expressed as the promotion of fair and just relations between the individual and society. Those who advocate for Social Justice specifically attempt to promote equality in society based on wealth redistribution, and by providing opportunities for personal activity and social privileges to the "oppressed." Essentially, it is the attempt to use government policies to break down barriers to social mobility, and to create economic equality. This process is pursued by manipulating taxation, social services, public health, access to public schools, access to public services, labor laws, and by regulating the market. All of this is done in the name of ensuring fair wealth distribution and equal opportunity for all.

As mentioned above, Social Justice is not about equal justice. Social Justice is based upon a relative standard. Those responsible for dishing out justice feel justified in being selective regarding who they deem deserving to receive benefits and sanctions. Based on their approach, it is their personal sense of "fairness," not justice, that is most important – and those in power get to decide what is fair.

Sadly, the standard of equal justice is not always applied in modern society. There are both societal and individual cases where people have not been treated equally under the law. It is because of that kind of injustice that some people advocate for "Social Justice." The thinking is that since some people have not received a fair shake in the past, out of "fairness" they should receive extra consideration in the future, while others should have their equal justice set aside.

The big problem with this is that you cannot create true justice by substituting a relativistic notion of "fairness" for justice. All it does is to change who is receiving unjust treatment.

As for the promotion of this movement within certain Christian denominations, the root of that is primarily found in various strains of liberal theology. While liberal theology tries to use the Bible to proof text its beliefs, the theology itself is not based upon the teachings of the Bible at all. Rather, the worldview foundation of these beliefs is right out of Naturalism.

As has already been noted, justice based on biblical values is established upon an objective standard that applies to all. Everyone, regardless of any outward circumstance, is measured against the same standard. This provides for genuine equality when it comes to applying justice.

A biblical approach does not involve trying to promote justice based on social factors. In order to promote true justice in society, it is necessary for there to be only one objective standard, and everyone must be held to the same standard. Then when there are cases where individuals or groups are receiving unfair treatment, the proper solution is not to try to right the wrong by disadvantaging some other individual or group. That only shifts the injustice to a different place.

The proper remedy is to hold the ones who are meting out injustice to account and make it right for those who have been treated unjustly. In the end, that is the only way true justice can be accomplished.

What Is Justice Really?

A few years ago at Oxford University in England, an event was planned to discuss the topic of abortion. This discussion was to be hosted by the pro-life group Oxford Students for Life, and led by two men, Timothy Stanley and Brendan O'Neil.

When a pro-abortion group got wind of the event, they protested loudly asserting that it was inappropriate for men to discuss if and when women should be able to make fundamental decisions about their own bodies. With that, the university canceled the event. Those who opposed it strongly defended the cancellation reasoning that, "The idea that in a free society absolutely everything should be open to debate has a detrimental effect on marginalized groups." They claimed that abortion is not an "abstract, academic issue," but one that affects women in a profoundly personal way.

One opposition organizer said, "In organizing against this event, I did not stifle free speech. As a student, I asserted that it would make me feel threatened in my own university; as a woman, I objected to men telling me what I should be allowed to do with my own body." She was asserting that limiting or eliminating abortion was an injustice to all women. While this particular event happened in England, the exact same thing, with the exact same reasoning, is common in the U.S., and in most other Western countries.

Of course, abortion is not the only Social Justice topic that is in vogue these days. The Black Lives Matter movement, along with the NFL player protests, objected to racial inequality in the legal system. The #MeToo movement was active against sexual harassment and other kinds of exploitation of women. Other popular Social Justice topics include income inequality, prison reform, gun ownership, transgenderism, gay marriage, and the list could go on.

The big problem when it comes to dealing with the topic of justice, however, does not relate to the fact that injustices exist. They do, and they should be addressed. Injustice should be eliminated wherever it is found.

The problem is not in the need to deal with it, but in how is it dealt with. Many of the prominent leaders of the Social Justice movement are not looking to right injustices as much as they are attempting to achieve their own personal political goals. This approach to dealing with injustice does not cure injustice, it creates more.

For instance, regarding the abortion story above, allowing abortion does not provide justice for those who want to have an abortion, and eliminating it does not create injustice. What is not taken into account (or even allowed to be debated) is the fact that every abortion ends the life of another human being who does not have a voice in the decision. The "justice" that the pro-abortion advocates want is a massive injustice to the innocent children that get murdered.

The same principle exists with all of the other social justice movements – every one of them. The reason for this is because the remedies these social justice advocates promote are completely one sided. They take an example of an injustice and generalize it to apply to everyone in a particular aggrieved group. If this principle were allowed to stand, it might very well eliminate the injustice that happens against particular individuals, but it would create its own injustice by penalizing people who have not committed any injustice at all.

Individuals cannot be legitimately deemed unjust simply because they happen to be a certain race or gender, or belong to some other identifiable group. This approach punishes some people who are not unjust and allows others who do commit wrongs to get off scot free – all because of some outwardly identifiable trait, characteristic, or belief. That approach does not produce justice.

There is a huge tendency these days to look at injustice through the lens of history. That should not be a problem when one is attempting to diagnose where problems exist. But it can be a huge problem if what happened in history becomes a means of generalizing a problem beyond what happened in history. It becomes a problem when a group is identified that has been historically "oppressed," and the remedy is designed to favor the descendants of that group at the expense of others.

This approach is based on a collectivist worldview philosophy that aims to favor the formerly disfavored group by disfavoring the formerly favored one. The problem is, you can't fix injustice or the injustices of history by creating injustice against others. The basis for creating true justice does not lie in a collectivist philosophy.

The only real remedy for injustice is to identify what it is and correct it. It is ultimately based on the rule of law where everyone receives equal justice under the law. This does not mean that those who are responsible for injustice should be allowed to avoid punishment, or that those who were on the wrong side of an injustice should not be appropriately compensated. But it does mean that you can't dole out punishment to those who are not responsible, and you can't assign responsibility to people who personally had nothing to do with a given wrong.

There is no doubt that getting to real justice can be a very difficult thing. In fact, there are some very serious problems we face as we try to root out injustice.

The first problem is that history is linear and we can't go back and undo what was done in the past. This means that there are historical injustices that will never be righted in this world.

A second problem is that we are not omniscient, and our limited knowledge and understanding makes it impossible for us to perceive all the factors that create injustice. The result is that regardless of how hard we try, we will never be able to right all wrongs. This is not a good thing, but it is a fact.

There is a third problem that is particularly serious – the problem of our fallenness. Sadly, there are a lot of people who don't want to fix the places where injustice lies. They gain an advantage from it, and the evil in their hearts compels them to ignore the injustices they see (or are a part of).

Because of these problems, we will never see perfect justice done on this earth. This does not mean we should not try, we absolutely should. What it does mean is that we must recognize our inadequacies and work to overcome them, all the while recognizing what Jesus himself acknowledged – that the poor ("the oppressed") will always be with us (Mark 14:7).

As Christians, we should always be working to right injustice. But we must also recognize that working towards that end does not correspond to our most important purpose on earth. The most important purpose is God's purpose – for all humanity to enter into a personal relationship with Him.

As such, our chief goal should be to lead people into a personal relationship with God. Righting injustice must be an "expression" of our Christian faith, not its "goal." If we focus on God's purpose, injustices will fall away.

The truth is, ultimately all injustices will be made right. Those who seem to be getting away with wrong will one day stand before the righteous judge and be put in their place. And those who have been wronged will be made whole by the only one who has the ability to create true justice.

In an ultimate sense, because of the limitations of our humanness and our fallen human nature, we do not have the ability to right all wrongs. We must do what we can, and with the right motives; but only God can ultimately fulfill justice. Our part is to align ourselves with God and see that, to the greatest degree possible, His will is done on earth as it is in heaven. The more that happens, the more we will see true justice prevail.

Love

Inserting the concept of love into a discussion about political matters may seem a little strange to some, but it's actually a very important theme when it comes to understanding the Christian basis of a democratic republic. Since the very concept of a democratic republic requires a focus on the individual, the essence of human life must be taken into account when building political structures to govern people.

Love is a spiritual concept that requires belief in a personal transcendent reality. If there is no personal transcendent reality, then the very concept of love is reduced to mere feelings that emerge purely out of physiological sources. If love is merely a physiological phenomenon, then there is no reason why it should be expressed one way rather than another. It becomes just another relativistic concept that must be defined based on the needs of the collective by those who have the power to enforce their ideas.

So the question becomes, are human beings persons made in the image of God who express love as an essential part of their personhood, or are they nothing more than physical animals that have feelings called "love" that are purely physiological?

Love from a Naturalistic Worldview (Collective, based on society's perceived needs)

Based on Naturalism, there is no such thing as a supernatural reality. That is, everything that exists is purely natural. So, when it comes to human existence, all that exists is the physical/animal element of a living creature, and feelings of love are viewed to be purely the result of chemical and electrical processes within the body. As such, there is no objectively real way that love should be thought of or expressed. Rather, as with all other areas, the purpose and proper expressions of love are considered to be based on the needs of the collective.

Beyond that, to the Naturalist there is no such thing as objective morality, so moral notions are also not a consideration in the way love is expressed. Morality, in Naturalism, is completely relative to the situation and the prevailing customs and conventions of a given social group. With that as a starting point, matters typically associated with love, such as what people believe about loyalty, marriage, and sex, are purely social constructs that can be thought of in any way society approves. There is nothing morally right or wrong, in an objective sense, with any form of sexual activity, and marriage is seen purely as a social institution that exists to serve society.

Love from a Christian Worldview (Individual, personal, based on the needs of others)

A Christian worldview defines the concept of love based on the teachings found in the Bible. It begins with the belief that human beings are more than mere physical animal creatures. They are spiritual persons created in the image of God who have a capacity for love and relationship that goes beyond physical attraction and interaction.

The biblical view of mankind, then, has its focus on the individual, not the collective. It is not that the collective is unimportant, but human value is based on individual existence first, which then translates into the collective as a natural result. God created human beings for the specific purpose of engaging in a personal relationship with each of them, and that relationship is established and expressed on an individual level. Beyond that, personal human growth does not have its purpose in the good it can do for the collective as Naturalists contend, but in an individual's discovery of and growth in God's purpose. God is the one responsible for protecting the collective, and He does it by guiding individuals, one by one, who then come together to form a fully functioning society (the collective) based on His purposes.

Using biblical beliefs as a starting point, the love that human beings show one another has a higher purpose; one that is found in the purpose and plan of God. Humans, then, are not working simply to promote survival and personal fulfillment, but to live and operate based on a personal purpose and calling of God, which is, in turn, based on the love of God and one's fellow human beings. Love's highest expression is found not simply in becoming a cog in a much larger wheel, but more importantly in the selfless giving of oneself. Each individual is admonished to give him or herself to God, and to others, in ways that demonstrate the love of God and express His purposes in their relationship.

This demonstration of love has an expression in public policy, as well. Since the primary object of love is God, public policy, with genuine love as a motivation, will always be based on beliefs that build up individuals and society. This kind of love puts the needs of others above self, and promotes such things as liberty, genuine justice, honesty and integrity, order in society, the value of marriage, and the value of life.

One illustration of this concept in public policy might be the passing of laws that protect people's freedom of conscience by not allowing them to be arrested for sharing Christ in front of an abortion clinic. Another example would be the implementation of laws and policies that protect children who are not able to protect themselves.

Why this Is Important in Governing

Human beings are persons, not biological machines. As such, the focus of governing should be on people rather than on governing systems.

Naturalistic beliefs, without exception, focus on system outcomes – in spite of the attempt of many Naturalists to assert otherwise. It can hardly be any other way. Even though many who try to govern based on naturalistic beliefs honestly think they are people focused, they are actually system focused. Their exclusive focus on what is best for the collective governs all of their policy decisions, and anyone who does not agree with them must be suppressed – for their own good, and for the "greater good."

Interestingly, people do express love no matter their worldview. That is because human beings are persons. That represents the actual structure of reality. Even people who try to govern based on collectivist worldview principles cannot help but frame their policy approaches in personal terms – even when the policies they promote have collectivist goals. What you end up with then are hybridized perversions that don't represent the way human beings actually operate in daily life. There is such a thing as objective reality, and that reality is that human beings have a built-in need and capacity for expressing love on an individual, personal level. Hybridizing that with collectivist policies only creates disorder and confusion.

Are There Values Necessary to Maintain a Democratic Republic?

So once again the question must be asked: Are the values associated with Christian Theism truly necessary for a democratic republic to work? And the answer is a resounding YES! Naturalistic beliefs and values simply cannot sustain the institutions of a democratic republic. Those values introduce unfairness and injustice into the mix that destroys fairness, honesty, and motivation – both at the societal and the individual level. That said, reversing the naturalistic trend is a massively difficult task because Naturalism is a religion, and people don't easily give up their religion.

But we can't have it both ways. We can't have the true and effective operation of the institutions of a democratic republic if they are not supported by the values that allow them to exist. There is a way reality exists and it does not exist any other way. It is incumbent upon every individual to examine their own beliefs to see how they align with reality, and to be honest enough with themselves to affirm what ought to be affirmed and change what needs to be changed.

How Public Policy Is Expressed Based on Different Worldview Values

Modern American liberalism is typically associated with politics, not with religion. That said, the worldview beliefs it is based upon is decidedly religious. Modern liberal beliefs have, as their worldview foundation, Naturalism – which is an atheistic faith system.

There are, of course, many people who consider themselves both Liberals and Christian, and it is at this point that we must make an important distinction. It is very possible for both Christians and non-Christians to hold beliefs that are detached from, or even opposed to, their core worldview. In fact, virtually everyone, including committed Christians, hybridize their beliefs to some extent and incorporate beliefs and behaviors into their lives that are not a part of the system they personally acknowledge. This often includes beliefs that are not even compatible with the beliefs they claim to hold.

Thus, there are many Christians who have incorporated modern western Progressive beliefs into the worldview they claim to follow without realizing that the origin of those beliefs are not from the Bible at all. At the same time, there are many who claim to be Atheists who display behaviors and/or work off of values that are directly opposed to Atheism – in fact, many even live by values they borrowed from Christianity.

The truth is, it is actually impossible to completely separate religious and political beliefs. Every outward expression of all belief systems have some philosophical underpinning that is, in its essence, religious. Our purpose here is to try to make a few fine distinctions as to how, specifically, modern western liberalism in today's American Democratic Republic relates to and is connected with naturalistic worldview beliefs. We will also include some insightful points from Christian Theism as a counterpoint that will allow us to make contrasts and comparisons.

Liberalism Is a Religious Belief

The first thing we need to understand is that modern American liberalism is not merely a political point of view. It has naturalistic worldview beliefs as its basic underlying foundation – and Naturalism *is* a belief system. In order to clarify this point, we will take a moment to point out the essential foundational beliefs of Naturalism. Then, to clarify it more fully, we will put it side-by-side with the essential foundational beliefs of Biblical Theism.

Liberal vs. Biblical Worldview Beliefs about God

- Liberal Belief – The natural universe, operating by natural laws, is all that exists. There is no God.

- Biblical Belief – God exists and He is the God of the Bible.

Liberal vs. Biblical Worldview Beliefs about Man

- Liberal Belief – Man is a naturally evolved animal creature and is essentially good.

- Biblical Belief – God created human beings in his image (His core essence is spirit), but mankind is fallen and in need of salvation.

Liberal vs. Biblical Worldview Beliefs about Salvation (the ultimate one can achieve in life)

- Liberal Belief – The ultimate one can achieve in this life is survival, and to attain the highest level of personal satisfaction possible.

- Biblical Belief – Salvation involves an individual's personal decision to enter into a personal relationship with God through faith in Jesus Christ.

Temporal Beliefs from Liberal Religious Beliefs

Obviously, the essential worldview beliefs above are not measurable using any kind of empirical system. Beliefs are, by their very nature, non-empirical and not subject to the tools of science. For this reason, both Naturalism and Christian Theism are faith (religious) systems.

There is another level of belief, though, that we also need to be aware of. While the essential worldview beliefs above are rather abstract, there are expressions of those beliefs that are slightly more concrete and can be outwardly expressed and measured in the lives of human beings. These are still beliefs, however, and not subject to empirical verification, even though they can be expressed more concretely.

- Liberal Belief – Since the natural universe is all that exists, everything can ultimately be understood by science. Thus, it is not necessary to pay attention to religion, and one can learn everything necessary to live in this world by science.

- Biblical Belief – Ultimate understanding comes from God's revelation. Thus, we can read the Bible and understand God and his ways.

- Liberal Belief – Man is a naturally evolved animal and not qualitatively special in the animal kingdom. Thus, there is no need to even consider God in the course of everyday life.

- Biblical Belief – Man is special in his ability to have a personal relationship with God. Thus, individuals can use human means to express this relationship.

- Liberal Belief – There is no such thing as objective morality; morality is relative to the situation. Since there is no God, there is no possibility for an objective moral code to even exist. Human beings must create morality for themselves based upon their particular life circumstances.

- Biblical Belief – Objective morality exists as a revelation from God. Thus, human beings should learn and follow biblical morality as it was given by God.

- Liberal Belief – The ultimate in life relates to this world, as there is nothing else. Life's ultimate purpose is survival; thus, individuals can only seek to do the best they can morally. There are no transcendent or eternal consequences for any particular human acts. The only consequences people may face as they live out their life are the effects that result from their actions in nature and those sanctioned by society.

- Biblical Belief – The ultimate in life relates to an individual's personal relationship with God – not only in this world, but for eternity. Thus, everyone should seek to know God and live in relationship with Him, because the consequences are forever.

Policy Expressions of Conservative and Liberal Religious Beliefs

There is one more level of human expression that comes into play. The previous two levels relate to beliefs only. The final level relates to specific actions that play out in the material world. These actions are not, however, independent of the beliefs mentioned above. In fact, they are direct expressions of them. People who genuinely hold biblical beliefs will act in accordance with those beliefs. Those who genuinely hold liberal beliefs will act according to their beliefs.

When it comes to political actions, it should be easy to see what policies will be promoted by people who hold various worldview beliefs. To make this abundantly clear, we will now take the actual policy positions and programs associated with liberalism and see how they are expressed. In doing that, we will also include a brief comment about the contrasting ideas that come from biblical beliefs in order to show the differences.

Individual Liberty Vs. Collective Control

The first category of liberal policy positions we will look at relate to who controls what goes on in society. Liberal beliefs are expressed as control over society by the collective (generally government) as opposed to the biblical belief of individual liberty.

Based on biblical beliefs, the individual has priority. It is understood that God created mankind for the express purpose of relationship with Himself, and that this relationship happens on an individual level. It is God's desire that all people know Him and live life based on His will and plan. If the masses of individuals do that, then society will automatically operate in ways that not only promote survival, but individuals will also experience fulfillment and fullness of life.

The priority of collective control emerges from the naturalistic belief that the physical universe is all that exists – thus, there is no afterlife. As such, survival of the species becomes the highest value, and it is believed that it is in the interest of the collective to maintain control of society to ensure its survival. Generally, it is considered that the government (or sometimes other collective institutions) should be the entity that has ultimate control in that regard. Therefore, it is up to government institutions to create and maintain policies that provide the best possibility for survival.

Liberal policies that operate on that basis include:

- Government support for unions (in order to use them as a means of collective control).

- Government support for social justice causes (ex. helping the poor, immigrants, minorities, etc.) These are all seen as efforts to ensure the survival of the collective.

- Promotion of sanctuary policies in relation to illegal immigrants – Sanctuary policies are understood to be an intermediary policy until a more complete "one world government" policy can be implemented. Sanctuary policies are a step toward implementing that goal.

- Government control of speech (allow only approved speech [ex. formally and informally sanction certain words and ideas] and the promotion of political correctness [ex. make laws to force non-complying individuals to act contrary to their conscience]) – The promotion of survival involves using all means necessary to eliminate conflict in society. One of the ways of doing that is to have everyone think the same way. Thus, beliefs that are contrary to what the collective deems to be correct need to be suppressed.

- Government control of information flow (ex. Fairness Doctrine, Net Neutrality, direct and indirect influence of social media) – Controlling the flow of information is another way of managing conflict in society to help promote species survival.

- Control of the judicial system (appoint judges with a liberal judicial philosophy) – A liberal judicial philosophy allows judges to make their rulings based on personal beliefs rather than on the intent of the law itself. By putting judges in place who prioritize the collective over the individual, order can better be maintained in society in a way that promotes survival.

Individual Vs. Government Responsibility

Another category of liberal policy positions relates to who is responsible for what happens in society. Liberal beliefs are expressed by the idea that the government has responsibility for overseeing the needs of those in society, as opposed to the biblical belief that it is the responsibility of the individual.

Based on biblical beliefs, every individual is responsible to God for their personal actions. God has revealed what is good and bad, right and wrong. So, based on the individual's personal relationship with Him, every person is responsible for accomplishing God's revealed purpose for their lives. This means individuals are responsible for earning a living and taking care of their own families and other responsibilities. If everyone does this, society will operate properly. This does not mean people should not help one other, but the helping should be done based on individual, rather than collectivist, principles.

The liberal concept is, once again, founded upon the naturalistic notion that the natural universe is all that exists, with its corollary belief that it is up to the collective to act as a "parent" to society in order to ensure the survival of the collective. As such, the government should properly implement policies that ensure this outcome.

Some of the particular policies that promote this end include:

- Promotion of minimum wage – It is considered that the collective is best served when everyone has a "living wage," and it is up to the government to regulate society in a way that ensures that outcome.

- Giving entitlements (ex. housing, food, childcare, elderly benefits, paid leave, retirement benefits, drug treatment programs, work programs, benefits to illegal immigrants) – It is believed that it is up to the government to make sure that people's basic needs are supplied, and this is best accomplished by government grants and subsidies.

- Control over education (ex. provide free schooling, provide subsidies for public education, eliminate private schools) – Education is seen as a means for providing society with the knowledge and skill base necessary to promote the survival of the collective. As such, the government needs to ensure that society's workers are adequately prepared. Public schools are also places where the masses can be indoctrinated in ways that reduce societal conflict. If everyone holds the same beliefs, the potential for conflict is reduced.

- Social engineering (government support for favored groups – ex. women, homosexuals, students, various minorities) – This is another place where the masses can be influenced in ways that reduce societal conflict. Again, if everyone holds the same beliefs, the potential for conflict is reduced.

- Creating business regulation to promote social justice causes – In addition to entitlements, government should advance policies that force businesses to support the kinds of programs that help promote the survival of the species.

- Nationalization of businesses – There are cases where it is in the best interest of the collective for important businesses to be owned and controlled by the government in order to best direct resources to promote the survival of the species.

- National control of law enforcement – There are cases where it is in the best interest of the collective for law enforcement to be controlled by the central government in order to best maintain order in society.

- Socialized health care (ex. Medicare for all, allowing only a socialized VA system, mandatory vaccinations and mask wearing, regulating drug availability, regulating and imposing particular insurance benefits) – As public health is an important category for promoting the survival of the collective, control of the health care system is understood to be an important government function.

- Human life. (ex. abortion, assisted suicide, and euthanasia) – Based on naturalistic beliefs, human beings are only one material animal on earth among many. There is no eternal or inherently moral aspect connected with the human species. As such, there is nothing wrong with controlling births and deaths if those overseeing the survival of the collective deem it a useful or necessary tool.

- Gun control – Controlling the availability of weapons is a legitimate government responsibility for the purpose of maintaining order in society and promoting the survival of the species.

- Promote the acceptance of homosexuals in society – Based on naturalistic beliefs, human beings are only material animals. There is no eternal or inherently moral element connected with the human species. In circumstances where there is deemed to be no negative impact on the survival of the species, moral taboos serve no purpose in society.

- Promote globalism (ex. foreign aid, redistribution of wealth from wealthy to poor countries, open borders, strengthen the UN) – The survival of the species is not viewed merely from the standpoint of individual governmental units (countries, states, etc.), but all human beings worldwide are considered to be a part of the species that need to survive. Ultimately, efforts need to be established worldwide to accomplish this end. The ultimate expression of this will be a "one world government."

Individual Vs. Collective Ownership of Property

A final category of Liberal policy positions relates to the nature of property and how it should be considered. Liberal beliefs are expressed by the idea that the collective should have the primary role in determining how property is controlled, as opposed to the biblical belief that the individual is primary.

Based on biblical beliefs, the primary principle that relates to the control of property is that of stewardship. The basic understanding is that God, as the Creator, is the ultimate owner of the entirety of His creation. However, He has assigned mankind to be his stewards (managers) in overseeing the created order.

As such, all individuals are responsible before God for the possessions that come into their lives – this includes all material possessions, including property. Under God's guidance, each individual is to manage his possessions in a way that accomplishes God's purpose. This, then, forms the basis for the principles of free enterprise and the private ownership of property.

The liberal concept is, once again, founded upon the naturalistic notion that the natural universe is all that exists, with its corollary belief that the collective has the responsibility to manage property in a way that promotes the survival of the collective. As such, the government should own, or at least control, all property and the means of production. This is primarily expressed in some form of Socialist or Communist government structure. Some of the particular policies that promote this end include:

- High individual and corporate taxes (ex. using taxes to steer the direction of the economy, wealth redistribution by taxing the rich) – Since the collective is responsible for the use and distribution of resources, it must collect enough from the work of individuals and businesses in society to effectively care for the needs of society.

- Heavy regulation of business practices (ex. benefits to favored businesses such as grants and regulation relief, benefits to favored organizations such as arts and humanities, benefits to favored government entities such as cities, states, and territories) – Since the interests of the collective take priority over the individual, it is up to the government to regulate business practices in ways that promote the greater good of society.

- Environmental control (ex. manage climate change, manage land development, inhibit resource development, control farming with subsidies) – As maintaining the earth's environment is important for human survival, the government has an interest in controlling the use of the land to promote the survival of the species.

Recognizing the Religion

As was mentioned above, modern American liberalism is viewed by most as more of a political philosophy than anything else. However, every political philosophy has an underlying worldview foundation that is a religious formulation, and liberalism is no exception. As such, liberal political policies are not mere political statements, but are religious statements based on beliefs that oppose Christian principles.

As a religious point of view, the tenets of liberalism have some very significant internal contradictions. These contradictions are expressions of the problems that emerge out of their view of science and morality. As liberalism is based on a naturalistic worldview with its belief that the natural universe is all that exists, it has no choice but to assert that natural laws govern every part of reality. That being the case, everything, in all of reality, must ultimately be discoverable and explainable using the scientific method. Thus, everything that cannot be explained by science must automatically be deemed as not real or untrue.

Beyond that, since Naturalism deems the natural universe to be all that exists, there is no possibility that God, as an objectively real person, exists outside of nature. As such it is not possible for any kind of objective moral beliefs to exist. Objective moral beliefs require an objectively real moral law giver, which Naturalism does not acknowledge. Thus, in liberalism, morality must be, by definition, a social construct made up by creatures that are capable of self-conscious thought – which on earth is only human beings.

Still, even for liberalism, there must be some basis for creating moral dogma – some underlying foundation. Based on the tenets of Naturalism, the bottom-line belief must be survival. All morality, then, must have, as its ultimate goal, the survival of the species. Since survival can be accomplished by different means in different situations, the moral expressions to promote that end can be quite varied in different populations, and it can even change in the same population if circumstances change. In other words, morality is, by definition, relative.

This brings us to the nature of the internal conflict we see in naturalistic belief – and by extension, in liberalism. Based on naturalistic (liberal) beliefs, the laws of nature are absolute; they do not change when circumstances change. On the other hand, morality is relative; it does change under varying circumstances. This creates a situation where the absolute nature of natural law and the relativistic nature of morality can come into conflict.

There are numerous quite profound examples of this conflict within liberal philosophy. For instance:

- The ultimate goal of naturalistic philosophy is survival, yet liberal policy actively promotes abortion on demand, and in some cases euthanasia.

- Naturalistic philosophy claims its ultimate authority source is science, yet liberalism denies that gender is binary (which is a scientific fact).

- Naturalistic philosophy is built upon an ultimate foundation of survival, yet liberalism promotes homosexuality that does not support procreation.

- Naturalistic philosophy claims science and survival as its bottom line, yet liberalism promotes environmental practices (particularly regarding forestry and water policies) that make the survival of humans in certain areas more difficult.

- Naturalistic philosophy touts human reason as its underlying approach to gaining knowledge, yet liberalism has no objective basis for doing reasoning (relativism promotes a "law of the jungle" mentality).

This list could go on using examples from almost all of the policy positions listed above. The point is, the absolute nature of Naturalism's understanding of material reality and its relativistic understanding of morality create an internal contradiction that mitigates against it actually representing the truth about how reality is structured.

Modern American liberalism is a religious faith, and it stands in opposition to the Christian faith – both in its underlying foundation and in its outward policy expressions. We cannot simply stick our heads in the sand and pretend liberalism is merely a political philosophy. It has political expressions, but it is, in its essence, religious. When liberal political expressions come to dominate a society, the ultimate result is disorder in the culture, and an assault against life, liberty, and human stewardship over life. And in the religious arena, it actively works to suppress Christian beliefs and Christian expression (as well as any other religious expression that opposes it).

Chapter 5

Does a Democratic Republic Truly Need So-Called "Christian Values?"

I
t feels like the political environment we find ourselves in today is as volatile as anything we have seen in modern history. Typically, when we think about the cause of the volatility, the matters that rise to the top relate to particular political policy issues. In

today's culture war, topics such as abortion, gay marriage, transgender rights, religion in the public square, gun rights, and others, are all trigger points in our political fights.

As Christians, we should not be passive bystanders in the political process. We need to be interested in the laws our politicians pass. And more importantly, we should never be mindless about how we engage the political process.

In fact, we need to be better informed, and to a much higher degree, than those who are not Christians. Of course, we must stand for the moral principles that are consistent with what has been revealed in the Bible, and we should promote public policy that is consistent with that. But there is more at stake here than mere political policy advocacy. The laws politicians pass create the overall cultural environment we must all live in.

And particular laws have outcomes that go well beyond the laws themselves. Those based on Christian beliefs protect individuals and society by promoting life and freedom. Those based on a naturalistic worldview platform – the other worldview system that is prominent in American society – promote an atmosphere that is ultimately hostile to life and freedom. Let's dive a little more deeply into this and take a brief look at what we are dealing with.

Policy Level

Policy pronouncements are outward expressions of inner human desires. Most who place their emphasis on the policy level end up advocating for their personal policy preferences without much thought about the underlying beliefs they are built upon. In this case, policies become an end in themselves. People who operate this way simply believe their position is correct, and fight for their preferences.

Unless a person has made the effort to understand their beliefs at the worldview level, this is almost unavoidable. That is why we rarely hear individual politicians, or the talking heads on TV, talking about "why" their position is correct. They generally just assume they are right and try to shout down their opponents. For these people, the policy is primary, and the reason for the existence of the policy, and its ultimate implications, are not considered important.

For those who make policy the primary focus, the policy itself is the goal. There is no thought of the larger consequences the policy might have for society. In these cases, politicians are thought of merely as policy makers.

Worldview Level

The worldview level goes much deeper and is the foundation policy rests upon. Everyone begins with a set of underlying worldview beliefs that, for them, are the basis for their understanding of morality, and the reason why they promote particular policies. The problem is, very few people are consciously aware of their underlying worldview beliefs. Worldview level beliefs are simply assumed to be correct. Then, based on those assumptions, individuals fight for policies that will promote the outcomes they deem to be right.

The Larger Environment

While most of the attention seems to focus on the policy level, in truth, politicians are much more than policy makers – they are culture and environment creators; even if they don't realize it. Every law that is passed not only creates some kind of regulation, it has a wider effect on the societal environment as a whole. Focusing on the larger environment is actually much more difficult than focusing on policy – because to do that a person must be able to see past the individual policy to its ultimate effect on society – which in some cases may take years to unfold.

In modern society, there are two powerful approaches being promoted that are in conflict with one another. One is based on an attempt to create a utopian society managed by government managers. The other seeks to create a society in which individuals are free to make their own way. These two approaches are diametrically opposed to one another.

As it turns out, the two major political parties in America have each aligned themselves with one of these two positions – which is why they are in dire conflict with one another. As we consider this idea, let's look for a moment at the underlying worldview beliefs that underlie these environmental possibilities.

Naturalistic Environment (Utopian)

The first potential outcome is that of a man-made utopia. The worldview system that seeks this kind of outcome is Naturalism. Naturalism is the belief that the natural universe is all that exists. Based on this belief, there is no God, thus there are no moral beliefs that can be considered objectively true. Man must create his own moral beliefs as he tries to establish a society that best promotes the survival of the collective.

Public policy from this perspective is not based on ideas that try to promote objective right and wrong, since that is not believed to exist. Rather, it seeks to promote stability based on the personal beliefs of those who hold power. Thus, public order and stability are not established based on what is in the hearts of individual citizens, but upon the enforced rules and regulations created by those who hold political power.

There is recognized to be no objective basis upon which decisions for society can be made. Everything is determined based on the beliefs and preferences of those who hold the levers of power. Individual freedom is set aside to accommodate the "greater good" as understood by those leaders.

Theistic Environment (Realistic)

The second possible outcome is based upon the rights of individual citizens who all believe in an objective right and wrong and are willing to follow what is right based on their own personal desires and decisions. These are people who believe that ultimately order in society emerges from an objectively real higher law that applies to everyone. This kind of environment is based upon a worldview system that is theistic, and believes God has revealed to mankind what is right and wrong. Politicians are charged with creating laws that correspond to what is right. Individuals follow the law, not because they are coerced by government authorities, but because they believe they ought to live by what is right.

The Environment Battle

These two different possible environments are battling today for supremacy in modern American society. If the environment based on naturalistic philosophy wins out, personal liberty will be shut down as those in power create rules and restrictions that limit freedom. If the environment based on Christian theistic beliefs wins out, order will be maintained in society, but will be based on the willing assent of the citizenry.

However, governing based on a Christian theistic approach does not guarantee that laws and policies will reflect Christian morality. What it does guarantee is that people will be free to choose their own way through the efforts of their elected officials, rather than be dictated to by government authorities.

For example, if the citizens choose to establish laws that do not correspond to a Christian understanding of morality, those laws will be upheld – not because they are morally right, but because the citizens have chosen them. At the same time, this approach does not allow political leaders to make laws that force Christians to violate their conscience. People must be free to choose to follow God (or whatever belief system they prefer), and laws must not be established which inhibit that.

By the same token, if Christian morality is codified and becomes the law of the land, this does not permit the "winners" to create laws where non-Christians are forced to violate their consciences either. In big picture terms, an environment based on Christian Theism must allow people the freedom to choose to go to hell if that is what they are determined to do. They just can't break civil and criminal laws as they take that path.

As should be evident at this point, the larger environment based on Christian Theism is not merely a policy driven process. The environment is bigger than individual policies, and policies must respect the environment. From my perspective, I would desire that politicians create public policy that is consistent with Christian morality. But the more important outcome, as it relates to civil society, is to provide an environment of genuine freedom where people's consciences cannot be violated.

The willingness to ensure that all people receive this kind of equal civil rights and freedom does not mean we agree with every law that will be passed, or that we should not exert great effort to create what we believe to be a moral environment by promoting policies that are consistent with Christian morality. What it does mean is that we respect other people as individuals as we try to persuade them in proper and respectful ways that promote freedom.

An environment, in itself, does not create success or failure. Individuals have to accomplish that on their own. That said, it does set people up for success or failure – not just in this life, but in eternity as well. As Christians, we care about the political and moral environment because we care about the people around us. We want people to live in an environment that gives everyone the best chance to succeed in this life.

The environment that exists in America is a democratic republic that was established upon Christian worldview beliefs. It is this set of beliefs that frees people, no matter their personal beliefs, to move forward in life based on the dictates of their own conscience. A naturalistic worldview platform does not provide for that freedom. If America is to continue into the future as a genuine democratic republic, Christian theistic beliefs must continue to be the platform that underlies our society's cultural environment and guides the nation. Without this, we will be ruled by the law of the jungle.

America has an unbelievably blessed political heritage. While that heritage certainly has, throughout its history, overtly expressed principles that are derived from the Christian faith, it is not merely the nod toward God where we see the beauty of what has been set in place. We also see a system that has a high view of the value of mankind – a view that cannot exist based on a naturalistic worldview. As such, every American, no matter their religious background, should fight to their last breath to pass that heritage on to succeeding generations.

About The Author:

Freddy Davis is the president of MarketFaith. He is the author of numerous books and has a background as an international missionary, pastor, radio host, worldview trainer, and entrepreneur. Freddy is a popular speaker, particularly on the topic of worldview and its practical implications for the Christian life. He lives in Tallahassee, FL with his wife Deborah.

Other books by Freddy Davis

The Truth Mirage

Shattering the Truth Mirage

Assaulting the Truth Mirage (Coming Soon)

Christian Worldview Commentary Series:

- Gospel of John

- Romans

- Galatians, Ephesians, Philippians, Colossians
- 1, 2, 3, John & Jude

www.freddydavis.com

MARKETFAITH
MINISTRIES

About MarketFaith Ministries:

You and your church could be on a transformative journey of faith with MarketFaith Ministries. In today's diverse and complex world, we understand the challenges Christians face. Our mission is to guide and empower you to live out your Christian faith with clarity and conviction in a world that is increasingly hostile to Christianity. Using our cutting-edge materials and comprehensive training, you will gain a profound ability to take Christ to what is now a massively pluralistic society. We can lead you to discover a renewed sense of purpose and confidence as you learn to authentically embody your faith and use that to make a positive impact in the world. Contact MarketFaith Ministries and let's partner together on a path that will lead to the growth of your church or business, and to a new level of spiritual depth for individual believers.

www.marketfaith.org